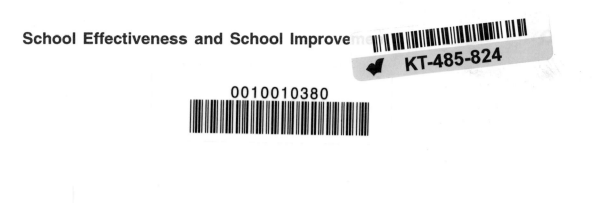

School Effectiveness and School Improvement

A Practical Guide

Alma Harris, Ian Jamieson and Jen Russ

PITMAN PUBLISHING

London • Hong Kong • Johannesburg • Melbourne • Singapore • Washington DC

PITMAN PUBLISHING
128 Long Acre, London WC2E 9AN

A Division of Pearson Professional Limited

First published in Great Britain 1996

© Pearson Professional Limited 1996

British Library Cataloguing in Publication Data
A CIP catalogue record for this book can be obtained from the British Library

ISBN 0 273 61622 6

10 9 8 7 6 5 4 3 2 1

Typeset by Phoenex Photosetting, Chatham, Kent
Printed and bound in Great Britain by Redwood Books, Trowbridge, Wiltshire.

CONTENTS

FOREWORD

This book has arisen out of work undertaken by the Centre for School Improvement at the University of Bath. The Centre has been engaged with local secondary and primary schools on a range of school improvement projects in recent years. In the course of our work we have become increasingly aware of the need for a text which makes accessible to teachers the rich store of research literature, case studies and experiences of school improvement. In part, this is a book which attempts to break down the divide between research and practice in the fields of school improvement and school effectiveness.

The responsibility for this book is shared between three authors. Ian Jamieson was responsible for drafting Part One on school effectiveness. Alma Harris, now with the Open University, drafted Part Two on departmental and classroom effectiveness. Jen Russ was responsible for researching and writing the case-studies which feature in Part Three.

A book such as this owes a number of debts to colleagues in the authors' own and other institutions. All three authors have worked on school improvement in the schools of the South Bristol Federation. They owe a considerable debt to these schools and to their co-ordinator, David Hunt. For their contribution to the case studies, particular thanks must be given to Linda Evans, Project Director of the Dudley Raising Standards Project, to Bernie Smith, Deputy Head at Four Dwellings School and Chris Owen, formerly Deputy Head at Four Dwellings School. Special thanks are also due to Christine Dean, who has acted as the secretary for this publication. Finally, we should like to thank our colleagues in the School Improvement Network (SIN) at the Institute of Education, London, for continual support and inspiration.

Alma Harris, Centre for Research in Teacher Education, Open University

Ian Jamieson and Jen Russ
Centre for School Improvement,
University of Bath

INTRODUCTION

It will perhaps come as a surprise to many teachers to learn that traditionally educational researchers have separated studies of school effectiveness from those concerned with improving schools. This book, alongside most recent research, attempts both to introduce teachers to the concept of an effective school and to show how effectiveness might be demonstrated, and to analyse the range of strategies which are used to help schools to improve. The book is not a definitive guide to research in the fields of school effectiveness and school improvement, rather it attempts to distil practical wisdom from these research studies in ways which practising teachers and educational managers will find useful.

Part of this emphasis on improvement has emanated from forces within schools; the determination of teachers to make sure that their schools do in fact make a difference to their children. Other pressures have come from outside the school, in particular from government. Schools, like many other organisations in the public sector, have been required to be more accountable to their various stakeholders, particularly parents. The publication of examination and test results and the introduction of parental choice have ensured that most schools placed improvement and effectiveness high on their agenda.

The book is divided into three parts. Part One concentrates on whole-school issues and considers what effectiveness and improvement mean in organisational terms. Part One therefore deals with the *macro* levels of organisational effectiveness and improvement, and examines how organisational change is effectively managed. Part Two concentrates on the level of the effective department, or faculty and subsequently upon the level of the effective classroom. Part Two, concentrates upon the teaching and learning issues associated with effectiveness and improvement.

Parts One and Two summarise and synthesise the key research and practical issues relating to school improvement and school effectiveness. Both draw upon the appropriate literature and refer to the separate research traditions. However, as the book is intended to be a practical guide, wherever possible, summaries of the research findings have been included in the text.

Part Three provides in depth case studies of school improvement. It focuses on both LEA-led and school-based initiatives at both the micro and macro levels of change. Illustrating many of the theoretical constructs covered in the previous two sections, it provides an insight into the ways in which some schools have endeavoured to bring about real improvement. Part Three also provides guidance for schools based on the case study experience.

We hope that schools will use this text as a way of accessing the wider research work referred to throughout Parts One and Two. In the 'References and Further Reading' section we have concentrated on texts which are both important and influential in this field. There is evidently much to be learned about school effectiveness and school improvement; we hope this book will provide schools with a useful starting point.

PART ONE

SECTION 1

School effectiveness

INTRODUCTION

It is difficult to think of anybody involved in schooling – parents, children, teachers, governors, LEAs and members of the local community – who would not be interested in schools being effective. This presupposes, however, that there is agreement amongst all these parties about what constitutes effectiveness. If we define effectiveness as being good at achieving the goals of schooling, we begin to see what sorts of questions we might ask about school effectiveness.

Two questions immediately present themselves: First, what sorts of goals do schools have, or should they have?; Secondly, do we have any ways of measuring to what extent those goals have been achieved, i.e. measures of how effective the schools are? Schools should find both of these questions useful even if the answers turn out to be more complex than they would like.

It may be that some of the stakeholders in a particular school have different views about what the school should be striving for. For example, the government and some parents may place most emphasis on academic results as measured by passes in public examinations. Other parents and probably a majority of the teachers may wish the school to pursue some broader objectives concerned with the development of a whole range of human capacities of which academic achievement is only one. As we shall see in Part Three, what seems important when it comes to objectives or goals is that the school does three things.

1 The school systematically tries to find out what most of its main stakeholders want from it. The views of parents, pupils and governors are vital here, but the interests of school staff and the wider community should also be considered.
2 The school takes a position on the multiplicity of goals which it could strive for, and is clear about its priorities.
3 Finally, the school needs to communicate these goals clearly and unambiguously to both its internal audience (teachers and other members of staff as well as its pupils) and its external audience (parents, LEA, members of the community).

Once this process of goal clarification has been completed, disregarding the argument that this ought to be a permanent dialogue with the school's various constituencies, then the school can begin the process of measurement. The term 'effective' presupposes that some sort of judgement or measurement has taken place, which indicates how close a school has come to reaching its goals.

Although it is perfectly possible to think of a school's effectiveness solely in terms of its achievement in relation to its *own* goals, in practice such a way of measuring effectiveness would be unusual. Most schools want their children to achieve a rather similar range of goals . They are, after all, members of the same society with similar demands to be made on them as citizens, consumers, producers, etc. Furthermore, most studies show that important stakeholders, like parents, have the same broad range of expectations from their schools. All this means that when we talk about school effectiveness our judgements are usually made on the basis of comparisons with other schools. It follows that in relation to any particular goal, e.g. academic achievement, or sport, or good behaviour, some schools will be judged more effective than others.

THE CONTEXT OF SCHOOL EFFECTIVENESS

Where does the interest in school effectiveness come from? This is not merely an academic question because the answers to this question will show practitioners where they might look for practical help in their efforts to improve their own institutions. It will be helpful to start with a diagram which shows some of the major influences on the thinking about school effectiveness (*see* Fig 1.1).

Effectiveness stream

There is a tradition of academic research, policy-making and professional decision-making that focuses directly on the question of school effectiveness. In this stream of work we can identify several important questions. The first is, *do schools make a difference*? If we assume that there are positive answers to this question, the second question will be, *can we measure the difference that schools make?* The final question is, *what then do effective schools look like?*

The first of our questions, do schools make a difference, needs some explanation. It is a question that was first asked in the context of a concern in the 1960s about the effects of schooling on social inequality.

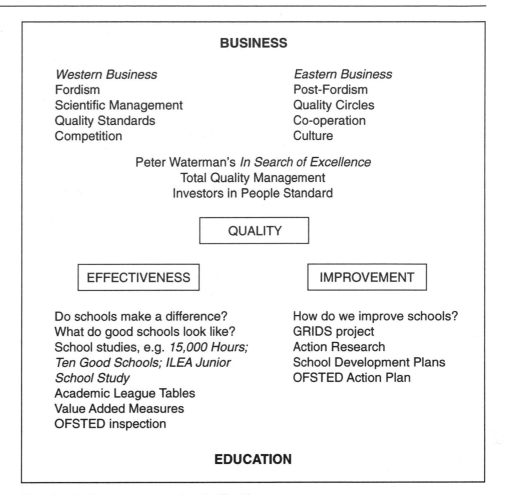

Fig. 1.1 Influences on school effectiveness

Leading American researchers like James Coleman (1966) and Christopher Jencks (1972) enquired whether going to school made any differences to the 'life chances' of children. Was it the case, for example, that in general, poor working-class children went to school but ended up being poor working-class adults, and that the children of the middle class ended up being middle-class adults? Both Coleman and Jencks, on the basis of large-scale studies, concluded that schools in fact made very little difference, that is, that a child's test scores or examination results could be predicted far more accurately from knowing the family background than from knowing which school the child went to.

There is little reason to doubt the general validity of these results. If we were to look at the aggregate results of GCSE examinations in

England and Wales, there is no doubt that parental background would be the best single predictor of performance. We can show this dramatically if we examine the recent results from one LEA in England – Nottinghamshire (*see* Fig. 1.2)

It is important to be clear about what is being asserted by such findings.

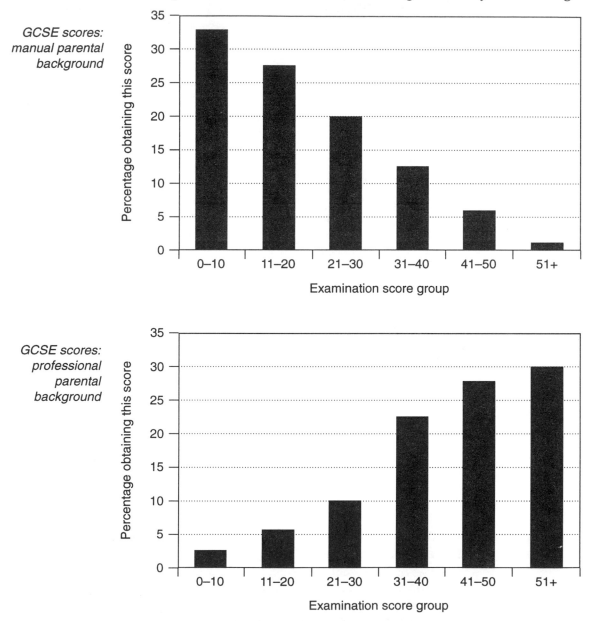

Fig. 1.2 GCSE scores and parental background in Nottinghamshire

Source: Jesson *et al* (1992)

What they show is that if you take large numbers of children and put them through an academic test or examination then any effect of the school they go to will be 'washed out' by the effect of their family circumstances, most particularly of the social class, i.e. occupation of their parent(s).

But let us look at another diagram produced by the Nottinghamshire researchers. In this scatter diagram the social class composition of the relevant year group in the school is used to predict how the children will perform at GCSE. The results should fall within the tramlines seen in Fig. 1.3, and as we can see the majority of schools perform as we would expect. However, we also notice two other groups of schools: the first performs significantly worse than we would expect, and the second performs significantly better.

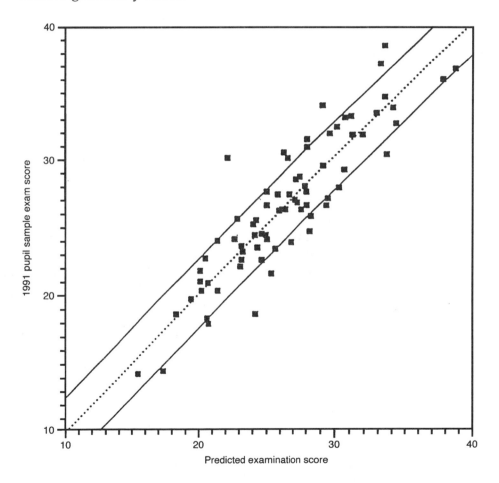

Fig. 1.3 School examination score versus predicted examination score from performance model in Nottinghamshire

Source: Jesson *et al* (1992)

This finding of variable school performance – the school effect – reflects a central tenet of the school effectiveness movement, namely that schools do make a difference. Such a finding replicates the results of one of the first and best-known studies of school effectiveness carried out in Britain. In 1979 Michael Rutter and his colleagues published *Fifteen Thousand Hours*, a study of twelve secondary schools situated in London, which showed that when you controlled for intake then on a range of student outcome measures these schools did differ from one another. Such findings are supported by a string of other studies, most notably *School Matters*, (Mortimore *et al*, 1988), a study of ILEA primary schools, and *The School Effect* (Smith and Tomlinson, 1989), a study of multi-racial comprehensives. These 'school effect' studies are replicated by work in other countries, particularly the USA and Australia.

It is tempting to see these studies as producing some form of 'recipe' for school effectiveness if we are measuring it by conventional academic performance. The Rutter study showed that effective schools were characterised by 'the degree of academic emphasis, teacher actions in lessons, the availability of incentives and rewards, good conditions for pupils, and the extent to which children are able to take responsibility' (Rutter *et al*, 1979, p 178). The study by Mortimore and his colleagues produced twelve key factors of junior school effectiveness which are widely reproduced.

In a different tradition to the researchers on school effectiveness were Her Majesty's Inspectors (HMI) and their LEA counterparts. Although most of HMI's work was on the inspection of individual schools, occasionally they commented on the general factors, which in their judgement, contributed to making a 'good school'. Their best-known publication is *Ten Good Schools* (HMI, 1977), which came to remarkably similar conclusions to *Fifteen Thousand Hours*. To HMI, the 'good school' is one that shows 'quality in its aims, in oversight of pupils, in curriculum design, in standards of teaching and academic achievements and in its links with the local community. What they all have in common is effective leadership and a "climate" that is conducive to growth' (HMI, 1977, p 36).

Although the mode of inspecting English and Welsh schools has changed with the creation of OFSTED (in particular, the inspections concentrate most closely on whether the various statutory requirements are being met) the publication of the *Framework for the Inspection of Schools* (OFSTED, 1992a, revised 1994a) and indeed the reports on individual schools clearly demonstrate that the model of the 'effective school' is alive and well, and indeed being reinforced by the OFSTED procedures.

Measuring performance

One of the distinctive features of the school effectiveness movement is their interest in making judgements, even measuring performance. The whole issue of trying to achieve an objective judgement of school performance is difficult, and this account will attempt to simplify an undoubtedly complex issue.

There are several key questions. First, how should schools develop criteria for judging effectiveness? Secondly, what are the criteria likely to be? Thirdly, who should be involved in making the judgements? We suggested in the introduction to this section that schools should consult their various stakeholders about their criteria for effectiveness and try to acheive consensus on a small number of key indicators. Much of the debate about school effectiveness pivots round a set of output indicators that are in the public consciousness and are, therefore, almost bound to surface in any discussion about effectiveness indicators. The indicators we have in mind are: examination and test results; truancy rates; staying-on rates in post-16 education (where relevant); destinations data. These are all output indicators in the sense that *to some extent* they are the result of what happens inside the institution.

There are two other types of indicators that institutions might consider. The first is a variety of what we might call satisfaction indicators, that is, an institution might wish to see whether the different constituencies which it serves are satisfied with both *what* the institution achieves and *how* it achieves it. Key constituencies here are the pupils and their parents.

The second type of indicator is directly concerned not with outputs but with processes, i.e. with teaching and learning. In order to make sensible use of process indicators it is of course necessary to have a robust model of school effectiveness in place. In other words, you must have a model which says that if the school does x y, z well, then it will be an effective school. The processes, (x y, z) are not necessarily valued in their own right, although they may be, but are valued primarily as a means to an end. An example at the level of the classroom might be having appropriate seating arrangements for the task in hand, or, more generally, actively engaging pupils in work tasks; at the level of the whole school, creating a climate or ethos which is focused on pupils and learning would be an example of a favoured process (*see* Section Four).

One can see immediately from these two examples that constructing process indicators presents quite a challenge to schools – on the face of it, it is easier to count the number of A–C passes at GCSE level. Although there are both conceptual and technical problems these can be overcome. The school effectiveness movement has provided us with some reasonably robust models of effectiveness on which we can work, and even concepts as difficult as school climate can be converted into some specific questions for pupils and teachers to answer.

'Value-added' measures of performance

One of the most common ways of measuring a school's performance is by its examination results. The reason for this is two-fold. First, most of the population believes that one of the prime functions of schooling is to impart knowledge, understanding and skills and that this is best assessed by some form of test or examination. Secondly, and linked to the first argument, the examinations are *public* examinations, i.e. the results are in the public domain, particularly so since the government has insisted on their publication in a certain format.

We have already seen, however, that a major determinant of the pupils' examination results is the socio-economic background of their parents. Researchers generally agree that something like half the differences in pupils' performances can be attributed to these background factors. John Gray and his colleagues, working with data from six LEAs, found that when differences in schools' intakes are taken into account, the differences between schools' results are roughly halved. 'We have seen this happen so frequently . . . that we have come to refer to this phenomenon as the "rule of half"' (Gray, 1993, p 28).

One can demonstrate this point if one examines the interesting graph produced by McPherson for the National Commission on Education (*see* Fig 1.4).

In view of these consistent findings it is clearly not very sensible to use 'raw' examination or test results to assess effectiveness, for either internal or external purposes. What schools want to know is: how effective have they been with the students they have in the school? It should be possible to refine this question further to: how effective have particular departments been in the school with individual students?; or even, how effective have individual teachers been with individual students?

The principle of answering these questions is relatively straightforward. Each institution requires a test or proxy measure of achievement on entry to the school and a test at the end to measure the 'value added'. Most schools use GCSE results at 16 as the output measure, but the measurement of achievement on entry is more varied. Some schools use socio-economic background of parents if it is known; others use IQ tests; most use some form of standardised verbal reasoning test.

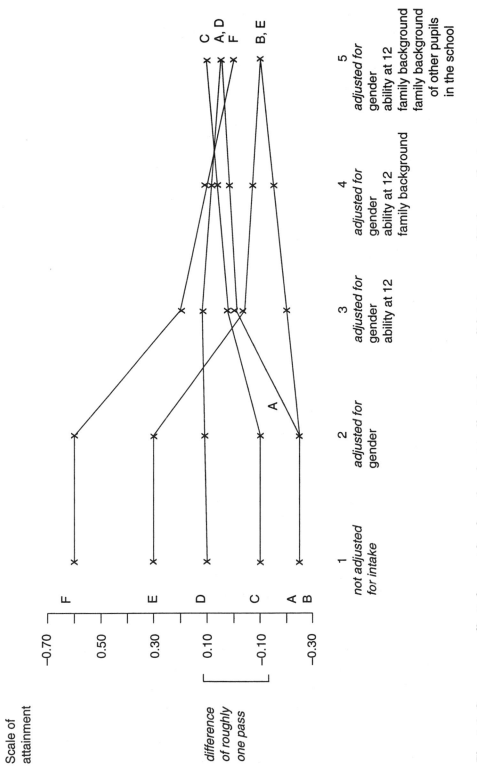

Fig. 1.4 Average pupil attainment in six schools unadjusted for pupil intake, and with four adjustments

Source: McPherson (1992)

OFSTED
inspections

If public examination results represent one of the public faces of school performance then OFSTED inspection results represent the other. Her Majesty's Inspectorate have always inspected schools to make judgements about their effectiveness and in recent times their reports have been placed in the public domain.

There were two main problems with these 'old style' inspections as an indication of a school's effectiveness. In the first place such inspections were relatively infrequent and did not represent the regular 'performance check' that schools might reasonably expect. For example, in 1987 less than one per cent of the total number of schools in England and Wales were subject to a full inspection. The second difficulty was that although there was considerable professional and public confidence in HMI as the authoritative voice of professional judgement on the performance of schools, the criteria by which judgements were made were often implicit rather than explicit.

The institution of new-style inspections under the OFSTED framework has lessened both of these problems. In the first place inspections are now to be carried out every four years for every school, although there must be doubts as to whether this very expensive operation will be continued indefinitely. More importantly, OFSTED have published the criteria which are to be used to judge school effectiveness in the *Handbook for Inspection of Schools* (OFSTED, 1992b, revised 1994b). One example is reproduced on pp 13 and 14. It refers to the criteria used by OFSTED to evaluate well-managed schools. It specifies the indicators for both satisfactory and unsatisfactory performance.

The OFSTED criteria necessarily take a formal and narrow view of school effectiveness; they are primarily concerned with the extent to which the school has complied with its statutory obligations, particularly with respect to the national curriculum. The 'conformance' model of effectiveness has its counterpart in some of the quality standards formulated in industry as we shall see (see p 18). At a national level it will probably be useful in raising minimum standards, particularly for low-performing schools. For other schools the observations of disinterested but knowledgeable outsiders will undoubtedly raise interesting issues about school effectiveness for school management to discuss.

OFSTED criteria for a well-managed school

Where a school is well managed:

- staff and governors have a long-term view of where the school should be heading. They take a systematic approach to the analysis of the school's current and future situation. Expectations are high and there are shared values and norms about learning, behaviour and relationships;
- the governors, headteacher and senior staff provide positive leadership which gives a clear direction to the school's work. Staff understand the role they are encouraged to play in the development and running of the school and also know that their contribution to the school is appreciated. Pupils learn effectively and efficiently;
- clear objectives and policies, focused on pupils' needs, are understood and implemented by staff and governors. The school development plan is a useful and effective management tool;
- The implementation of plans is monitored; problems are identified early and where possible resolved. Finance is efficiently managed and focused on clear priorities for the provision of resources;
- administrative procedures and daily routines are well established. Day-to-day decisions are regarded by staff, parents and pupils as being fair and consistent;
- governors, staff, parents and pupils have a strong commitment to the school. Roles and responsibilities are clearly defined and there is appropriate delegation;
- governors, staff, parents and pupils are clear about communication routes within the school and feel that these operate effectively. The head and senior staff are accessible and approachable;
- firm arrangements for periodic reviews exist. Performance indicators (or 'success criteria') are used and comparative information sought. Lessons learned are fed back to staff and governors and into the school's planning process and the school's goals are re-evaluated.

Source: OFSTED *Handbook* (1994), p 63.

OFSTED criteria for evaluating poor management of a school

Where management of a school is unsatisfactory:

- staff and governors have little long term vision for the school. There are serious discrepancies between the values stated by staff and those implicit in actions or behaviour of staff or pupils;
- staff feel their contribution to the school is not appreciated. Pupils' learning is ineffective or achieved inefficiently. Standards achieved do not adequately reflect the pupils' abilities;
- the school development plan is not based on any assessment of needs. Specific plans are unrealistic or badly constructed, and adequate resources are not provided for them. Aims and policies have little effect on practice;
- inefficient co-ordination of decisions and actions limits effectiveness and leads to inadequate performance and the poor deployment of resources, including staff;

- the administrative framework is disjointed and ill-planned, or excessively detailed and obtrusive. Senior staff are not around the school enough to notice what is going on, or to resolve problems;
- staff and governors are not clear for what they are responsible. Decisions are taken without proper participation and consultation;
- governors, staff, parents and pupils complain about inadequate communications. The head and senior staff may be remote or unapproachable;
- evaluation and review is absent or ineffective. There is little use of performance indicators or comparative information. There is no provision to feed back any lessons learned into the planning process.

Source: OFSTED *Handbook* (1994), p 64.

School improvement

INTRODUCTION

The majority of schools which have been through an OFSTED inspection believe that the observations of the inspection team have been useful and could provide an incentive to school improvement. However, the OFSTED model adheres firmly to the school effectiveness school of thought, that is, it makes a judgement at one point in time about how effective the school is when judged against certain criteria. The criteria themselves are derived more from interpretations of pieces of relevant legislation or guidance than from models of school effectiveness. A frequent complaint of OFSTED inspections is that they do not of themselves help schools to improve.

The stream of work coming from the *school improvers* attempts to help schools with the process of improvement. The definition of school improvement adopted by the International School Improvement Project (ISIP) is a useful starting point. They define school improvement as 'a systematic, sustained effort aimed at change in learning conditions and other related internal conditions in one or more schools, with the ultimate aim of accomplishing educational goals more effectively' (Van Velzen *et al*, 1985). More prosaically, we might employ a definition which saw improvement as 'a systematic attempt to enhance teaching and learning which has its focus both in the classroom and in the school'.

Work in the field of school improvement centres around three key ideas or concepts: reviewing and evaluating; change and innovation; action research and action learning. Any school improvement initiative tends to involve elements of all of these strategies.

School improvement nearly always starts with a view or an evaluation of some aspects of a school's functioning. This could be the OFSTED inspection which is a form of evaluation. A good example of this approach is the Guidelines for Review and Internal Development in Schools Project (GRIDS). This School Council project was one of the first to codify a useful model for school review. The principles which GRIDS adopted have been influential in a number of subsequent developments. We might define them as follows:

- Consult widely on what issues to concentrate on.
- Agree what sorts of data would be relevant to the issue.
- Collect data.
- Review data collectively and let improvement strategy emerge.

Such a model can be interpreted in simpler language:

- Where are we now?
- Where do we want to get to?
- What do we need to do to get there?
- How will we know when we have got there?

MANAGEMENT OF CHANGE AND INNOVATION

School review and evaluation are always done with a purpose and that purpose is to improve the school. School improvement involves change, *planned* change. Whereas all improvement involves change, not all change is necessarily an improvement. The school improvement literature draws heavily on ideas, concepts and strategies of the management of change, in particular on the work of M.G. Fullan (1991), Louis and Miles (1990), and Miles (1986).

School development planning

A specific feature of the improvement process, which has now become a statutory requirement for schools in England and Wales, is the school development plan. The development plan attempts to codify much of what we have learned about the process of improvement.

- It institutionalises a regular planning and review sequence.
- It sets targets and costs them in terms of resources.
- It is ideally based on the assessment of information from previous reviews.
- It should reach every level of the organisation so that it has an effect on teaching and learning.
- Its construction and review are collectively undertaken.

School development plans can be a useful tool for school improvement but as Mortimore shows, like all other tools they offer no magic solutions – the mere existence of a plan guarantees nothing [Mortimore,1995].

Action research and action learning

Another strategy used by the school improvement movement is action research. We can define action research in the context of school improvement as a systematic attempt to learn about what strategies improve schooling by the careful monitoring of significant innovations. This can be summed up in the popular PLAN—DO—REVIEW refrain, or seen more graphically in the action research cycle (*see* Fig 2.1).

Such a model seems well suited to school improvement with its focus on trying out schemes and reviewing their effect in a systematic way. It is also closely linked to the *teacher as researcher* movement pioneered by Lawrence Stenhouse (1975), as well as to the idea of the *reflective practitioner* (Schon, 1983) which is highly influential both in education and in other professional fields.

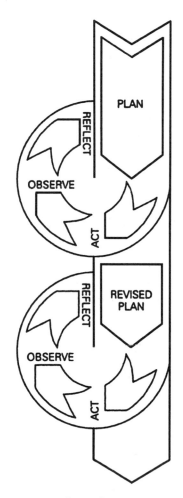

Fig. 2.1 The action research cycle

QUALITY AND THE BUSINESS INFLUENCE

The school effectiveness and school improvement models are firmly rooted in education, but there is another source of influence on schools that aims to improve effectiveness, namely the business world. The pivotal concept here is that of *quality*, although this is a term which has only recently come into focus as the guiding concept.

There are two main reasons why business practice has had an impact on ideas about school effectiveness. The first can be traced back at least as far as the turn of the century when the revolutionary benefits of industrial mass production and accompanying business organisation began to be realised on a significant scale. From this point on, particularly in the United States, there arose a view which suggested that business people knew best how to organise and manage things. It is certainly the case, for example, that until relatively recently texts on educational management have drawn very strongly on the literature on business management (*see* Everard and Morris, 1990). The other reason for business influence on educational thinking about effectiveness is the changes which have been brought about in recent years in the organisation of schooling, in particular the attempts to bring schools into the market-places, which have been made through such measures as the local management of schools (LMS) and open enrolment. To the extent that these changes have been successful, the effect has been to make schools much more like businesses. All organisations in the market-place face pressures to hold or increase their market share, satisfy their clients, budget effectively so as to minimise their costs, etc. This means that, perhaps for the first time, there are some real similarities between the tasks of school/college management and those of other organisations. If this is true, or thought to be true, then the transfer of ideas and practice between sectors has significant potential.

The Western business tradition

We want to argue that there is not one set of business influences on effective schooling, but two. For the sake of simplicity we have described these as the Western and the Eastern business traditions. The West, until relatively recently, has been dominated by models of management that have emanated from the management of mass manufacturing. Such manufacturing is epitomised by the techniques first pioneered by the Ford Motor Company and is appropriately known as Fordism. Closely associated with such models is the tradition known as *scientific manage-*

ment. Although the term is a slightly old-fashioned one, the ideas are still important. The notion of scientific management is derived from the idea that what is to be done and how it is to be done is best achieved by a close study of the problem by experts. This view of management implies that once the experts have decided on the system then it is management's task to make sure that people inside the organisation conform to the specification. The whole model can be seen in the operation of something like time and motion study.

The application of this philosophy in modern times can be seen in the development of *quality assurance* models. The best-known of these standards is BS 5750, now known as BS EN 1S0 9000. Quality assurance models concern themselves with making sure that the correct procedure for undertaking certain tasks is being followed. Quality in this sense then means conformance to a standard or specification. In formal systems of quality assurance, such as the BS EN 150 9000 standard, conformity to the procedures is checked by a third party who acts the role of auditor. If a school or college attained the standard it would be subject to six-monthly checks on its systems and system use by a registered certification body, e.g. Lloyds.

Although these quality assurance models were developed in an industrial context (from NATO procedures for commissioning equipment from industry), they are in principle applicable wherever there is a desire for employees to follow routine procedures. If we think about the context of schooling then there are a number of tasks that might be suitable for the quality assurance treatment. These might include:

- financial management
- admissions
- issuing statements
- induction of new staff
- dealing with parents
- curriculum review

Where a quality assurance model is in place this nearly always results in the production of a manual of procedures.

The passing of the Educational Reform Act in 1988 and the ensuing national curriculum paved the way for some sort of quality assurance model to penetrate the curriculum area of schooling. There is some sense in which OFSTED inspections resemble quality assurance models because they are largely concerned with ensuring that schools are complying with the national curriculum and other associated legislation. OFSTED inspections are more than just exercises in quality assurance, however; they do make an attempt to judge substantive quality. The difficulty with quality assurance models is that they can only testify that the correct procedures have been used, and these may be a necessary condition for quality education, but are not sufficient in themselves.

A similar approach to quality assurance has been adopted by the government with its system of *charter marks*. To obtain a charter mark, an organisation has to demonstrate that it is systematically and routinely achieving certain standards of service to all its 'customers'. These include the following:

- publication of standards of service and performance against those standards
- customer consultation
- clear information about services
- courteous and efficient customer service
- complaints procedure
- independent validation of performance and a commitment to value for money

There is of course a well-known issue in schooling about who constitutes the 'customer' (a phrase not much liked or used in education). In secondary schools in particular there is clearly a discussion about whether the clients or customers are the students or their parents. Notwithstanding this discussion, the ideas behind charter marks usher in a new way of trying to improve effectiveness—using consumer or market pressure. This is very much in line with the philosophy behind markets which underpins much government thinking and which is ultimately derived from the business world—the idea that competition and consumer pressure can force organisations to be more effective. Certainly one can argue that if parents or pupils know the service standards, and know what the routes of redress are, then, all other things being equal, this could have the effect of pushing up standards of service. Whether this affects the quality of schooling is another matter. It might be argued that its effect could be indirect but nonetheless important. For example, if parents were very satisfied with the way in which they were treated by the school they might be much more inclined to enter into some partnership agreement with the school to support the work of their children, and so directly influence one of the factors which the school effectiveness movement has pinpointed as important (*see* case study C, p 137).

An example of a service guarantee approach can be seen in the work of Berkshire LEA, part of which is reproduced below:

Primary and Secondary Schools

- We guarantee to let parents request a place for each child at the school of their choice, to provide a place at that school if available, and to provide the right to have the case considered by an independent body if a request is turned down.
- We guarantee to provide clear, easy to read information about education in Berkshire, and clear comparative information about all schools available.
- We guarantee to provide regular written reports on each child and annual meetings with each child's teacher to discuss their progress.
- We guarantee parents can elect representatives to the governing body of their school, or stand themselves.
- We guarantee each school will produce an annual report, and that parents can discuss the report and any matter concerning the school with the governing body.
- We guarantee that children will be well taught, well cared for and treated fairly at school.
- We guarantee to provide parents with the right to complain and have complaints heard impartially.
- We guarantee that no child will be excluded from school other than for good reason. Parents will have the right to appeal against any decision to exclude a child for more than five days, and to have the case heard by an independent panel.
- We guarantee to assess a child for special educational needs where there is good reason.
- We guarantee parents may meet inspectors during any formal inspection of their child's school, and can request copies of inspection reports and governors' proposed action plans for any school.
- We guarantee to provide free meals for children of families who receive Supplementary Benefit or Family Income Support. Children over 16 attending a Berkshire school or college may also receive financial assistance.
- We guarantee to provide free transport for 5–8 year olds if their local school is more than 2 miles from home and for 8–16 year olds if their local school is more than 3 miles from home.
- We guarantee to arrange transport for students under 19 years old attending a maintained school sixth form or a full time college course within Berkshire for a fixed charge of £270 per year, irrespective of distance.
- We guarantee to provide transport up to a maximum value of £115 a

term for children attending their local denominational school if the school is:

—between 2 and 6 miles from home (5–8 year olds)
—between 3 and 6 miles from home (8–16 year olds)
—over 3 miles from home (11–16 year olds).

The Eastern business tradition

We have characterised the Western business tradition as being primarily concerned with effectiveness by relying on the forces of competition, and by instituting a system of management-led procedures and structures. This of course is a broad characterisation and only makes sense for comparative purposes. Our point of comparison is what we have called the 'Eastern business tradition'.

The influence of this tradition, emanating from Japan but now embracing many of the countries of the Pacific rim, came about because of the astonishing post-war success of its economy. If one examines some of the feature of this success in terms of the structures and processes of the companies, a different model of effectiveness begins to emerge. This model exhibits some of the following features:

- Organisation structures tend to be rather flat and not so marked by hierarchical divisions.
- Tasks are organised in a flexible way and the division of labour is de-emphasised.
- There is an emphasis on teams rather than individuals and co-operation within the organisation rather than competition.
- There is an emphasis on the culture and values of the organisation.

This rather different business tradition has had an influence on our ideas of effectiveness. The Quality Circles movement is a good example of an idea which is directly derived from Japanese business practice and which has had an influence not just on Western business but also on education. The Quality Circles approach to improvement is marked by the following characteristics:

- The formation of an *ad hoc* group, marked by equality, to help improve the effectiveness of a particular area of work.
- The group work together as a team.
- The mission of the team is continuous improvement.
- The group uses a range of techniques to examine both performance and to suggest improvements.

Apart from specific 'imports' like Quality Circles, the more general ideas of Eastern business have strongly penetrated the Western world. Many of these ideas were given a strong impetus by the publication in 1982 of Peters and Waterman's *In Search of Excellence* (Peters and Waterman, 1982). This book was a study of a significant number of America's best-run companies as measured by the normal criteria of business performance. Although controversial because of its methodology, and because many of the companies did not manage to sustain their performance in subsequent years, the book had a very significant effect on management thinking about effectiveness. Although the study was of US companies, in fact the eight principles of effectiveness were much more features of Eastern than Western business. It is not difficult to see how these eight features can be applied to schools.

- *A bias for action:* realising the limits to solving problems through planning round the table; having a preference for action research models.
- *Close to the customer:* effectiveness comes through attending closely to the needs of pupils and parents.
- *Autonomy and entrepreneurship:* teachers should be given as much autonomy as possible and should be encouraged to be innovative.
- *Productivity through people:* improvements largely come through people not procedures. Schools should emphasise trust over control and should systematically reward effective behaviour.
- *Hands on, value-driven:* the school should have a clear mission and goals underpinned by an explicit set of values which is shared by all.
- *Stick to the knitting:* schools should concentrate on their core task— teaching and learning—and not be distracted by other activities.
- *Simple form, lean staff:* simple, flattish organisational structures work best with few strata of hierarchy and the minimum of rules.
- *Loose–tight properties:* the school should specify tightly the minimum key elements of its work that need to be followed and then teachers should be given the freedom to work within this framework.

Once these principles have been translated into a set of precepts which make sense to schools then a remarkable overlapping with the work of the effective schools movement can be noted (*see* Section One) .

The publication of *In Search of Excellence* drew attention to a number of management theorists who were interested in the 'soft' variables of effectiveness like 'culture' and 'people'. In particular, there was an ever-growing interest in the ideas of effectiveness and in a concept of growing importance—*quality*. The work of Deming in particular became influential. Although Deming was an American, most of his early work on quality had been taken up and used by Japanese companies, but with the growing influence of these firms and the attendant increasing interest in their methods, the work of Deming (1986) and of writers like Crosby (1986) and Juran (1979) became ever more influential.

The main influence of these writers is on the movement known as Total Quality Management (TQM). TQM is a philosophy rather than a system, with the following major features:

- Quality is largely defined by the customer.
- Customers should be seen as internal to the organisation as well as external. For example, teachers are customers of in-service training; pupils are customers of teaching; administrative personnel are customers of teachers for pupil data, etc.
- We improve by a process of continuous improvement—a never-ending process.
- Although quality might be insisted on by senior management it is everybody's responsibility: TQM cannot be delegated.
- The focus of TQM is prevention of problems, not detection.
- Decision-making is based on hard data about performance.
- Teams are the most powerful agents for delivering quality.
- Productivity is through people—human resources must be valued, trained and developed. The climate or ethos of the organisation is vital.

Many schools have become interested in these various quality initiatives, although it should be clear that the choice of an initiative based on the Western business tradition or on the Eastern, will make quite a difference to the type of initiative, which does not mean that something like BS EN 1S0 9000 is necessarily incompatible with TQM (*see* Peters and Waterman's (1982) loose–tight properties of organisations).

A particular initiative which many schools and colleges have become committed to in the last few years has been the *Investors in People* standard (IIP). This is a quality standard which focuses on human resources, particularly training. Introduced in 1990 and initially devised by the CBI, it was developed by the National Training Task Force which has been charged with improving the quality of training in Britain. This quality standard for training is operated through the Training and Enterprise Councils (TECs).

The Investors standard has proved a popular initiative with educational organisations; this is probably so because of its focus on people in organisations which spend 80 per cent of their budget on staff. The key features of IIP are:

- Organisations are to develop a clear view of their mission and goals.
- A public commitment to develop *all* employees, i.e. teaching *and* ancillary staff.
- A regular review of the training and development needs of all staff throughout their employment.
- Evaluation of training and development regularly undertaken against benchmarks to ensure future success.

CONCLUSION

The thesis with which we began this contextual overview was that a wide range of different traditions are beginning to converge on the theme of effectiveness and quality. These include models which have been derived from within the educational circles—school effectiveness and school improvement; and models which bridge the educational—business divide, like action learning and action research. Schools and colleges have also drawn from the business world: from models which stress the power of markets and competition to improve performance, to those which stress the benefits that can be gained from a focus on quality assurance procedures, and attention to the culture and values of the organisation. There is a sense in which these various models show us the multi-faceted nature of school effectiveness and improvement. Different schools have been attracted by different facets of these various programmes, their selection doubtless influenced by the perceived needs of their own institution, which tradition is locally visible and available, and which intuitively appeals to school decision-makers.

All these initiatives can be presented in many different ways and our diagram (Fig. 1.1) on p 5 shows how we see them. More conventionally we might see them as either emphasising the *promotion of quality* or the *assuring of quality*. In promoting quality the emphasis is likely to be on things like:

- TQM.
- School development planning.
- Staff development (perhaps through the IIP standard).
- Examples of 'good practice'.
- Setting performance standards.

In assuring quality the emphasis is likely to be on the following:

- Developing performance indicators of quality for both processes and outputs.
- BS EN 1S0 9000.
- Value-added analysis, e.g. QUASE, ALIS, YELLIS systems.
- Monitoring and evaluation.

Effective schools are likely to embrace the twin objectives of both improving and proving quality.

Managing the effective school

INTRODUCTION

The various studies of effective schools usually display similarities in terms of their management and organisation, and it is tempting to believe that there is some sort of 'recipe' for effective schooling. In fact what we have is some findings which suggest interesting correlations between schools which manage to perform well in conventional academic tests or examinations, and certain features of their management and organisation. Furthermore, these features of management and organisation of successful schools should be seen more as indications of the right direction than as prescriptions for the management of effective schools. Schools are highly complex organisations with a constantly changing group of pupils; in such a situation effective management will always be a question of checks and balances and nuances of action which will combine together in complex ways. The best that any guide like this can achieve is to suggest those management strategies that, in general terms, are most likely to make a school effective.

VISION, MISSION AND GOALS

Effective schools are marked by a clear sense of purpose that is shared by all the members of the school. This sounds straightforward but in fact it is a complex aim and is rarely achieved by any organisation. It is useful to distinguish between vision, mission and goals.

Vision

A vision statement tries to sum up what the school is trying to achieve in a brief and memorable way. Murgatroyd (1992) describes them as 'powerful touchstone statements'. The function of the vision is to guide the school, to signal clearly what it is trying to achieve. A powerful example we have come across in an all-girls school is 'To help every girl to become her own woman'.

This really is a touchstone statement which clearly encapsulates the vision of the school. The whole point of vision statements, if they are to have any meaning is that they should act as a clear guide to behaviour, that is, they should allow people to decide between alternative courses of action. Schools very often spend large amounts of time talking about the *values* they believe in and wish their pupils to adopt. Such conversations only become really useful and linked to ideas of effective schooling when the values are clearly linked to desired behaviour, on the part of teachers, pupils and other school employees. Because values can be elusive things to talk about, not least because the language of values can prove to be difficult (democracy, freedom, truth, etc.), some schools often find it more useful and practical to talk about desired behaviour first as a way of identifying the values which are important to them.

Murgatroyd (1992) suggests that good vision statements are those which pass the following tests:

- The vision statement makes clear what the school's priorities and commitments are
- The vision statement provides a torch and a touchstone—it is a statement that can be used repeatedly to inspire, encourage and evaluate
- It is a statement that can be used to re-focus energy when energy is being dissipated
- It is a measure by which the school wishes to be judged
- It excites, inspires and concentrates the minds of those associated with the school

Mission

Vision statements need to be short and memorable so that they can have real 'bite' or weight in the institution. It follows from this that one cannot say anything very much in such a statement. The mission statement is the expansion of the vision statement in which it is possible to say in some detail exactly what it is the school is trying to achieve. Mission statements often include some or all of the following:

- Some statement about the purpose or aims of the school, e.g. the aim of John Brown school is to prepare well-rounded citizens who are able to play a full part in the life in the community.
- Some statement about the commitment of the school to certain standards or values, e.g. a commitment to develop talent in all children.

- Some statement about the values which the school stands for, e.g. tolerance and respect for the views of others.
- A statement about the unique, or special features of the school, e.g. a musical or sporting tradition which is of particular importance.

The difficulty with mission statements in many schools, or more realistically with the school aims which are reproduced in the school prospectus, is that they are wordy and lack any real meaning inside the organisation. Mission statements will only lead to improvement in schools if they are seen to be useful. Murgatroyd and Morgan (1993) specify some criteria to which they believe mission statements should measure up.

- Challenging: always in sight, but not out of reach.
- Clear: not open to conflicting interpretations by any group or individual.
- Involving: a statement that enables and empowers all.
- Value-driven: a statement that is clearly connected to the desired values.
- Visual: something that can be represented or pictured visually.
- Mobilising: something that should demand a response from everybody.
- Guiding: something by which everybody in the organisation can measure their actions.
- Memorable: something that can be easily reproduced from memory.

Goals

The common difficulty with vision and mission statements in the context of schooling is that they do not make a sharp enough impact on the behaviour of individuals inside the school. The failure is ironic given that this is their main purpose. There are a variety of reasons for this failure. First, the statements are not clear and sharp enough; second, they have usually been constructed without the co-operation of members of the school; thirdly, there are far too many of them so that they lose their effect; finally, they have not been translated down to the level of the individual so that they have real *personal* meaning.

A focus on objectives in the school represents an attempt to translate the mission of the school into action plans. This does not mean that all elements of the mission necessarily have to take the form of objectives all the time. It is more likely to be helpful if, say, departments or pastoral teams decide to re-focus energy on particular objectives which they believe are not being fulfilled at the time.

The management literature indicates that the most effective objectives are SMART. The SMART acronym is translated in the following way:

S—Specific: objectives should be as focused as possible.

M—Measurable: objectives should be capable of being measured in some way so that it is possible to judge if they have been achieved.

A—Agreed: objectives which are imposed on others rarely motivate.

R—Realistic: the goal here is to set objectives which cause people to work at full stretch but which are achievable.

T—Time constraint: there needs to be a time limit for the achievement of specific objectives.

Constructing vision, mission and goals

We have argued that a key element in effective schools is the clarity of the goals they set themselves But clarity is not everything; for the goals to have an effect on the behaviour of teachers, support staff and pupils inside a school, there must be agreement on the goals. One of the best ways of securing that necessary agreement is to involve people in the construction. One of the big advantages of the Investors in People approach (*see* pp 24–25) is that it systematically involves *all* the employees of the school, support staff as well as teachers. It is more difficult to involve pupils because of age and maturity considerations, plus the fact that they are transient members of the school. The practice which schools have found most useful is to involve their stakeholders, i.e. parents, governors, representatives of the local community, as well as their employees, in an exercise on the vision and mission, and then to involve pupils in the setting of specific objectives for the term, year, etc.

Conclusion

We began this section by asserting that effective schools are marked by clarity of goals. We have tried to elaborate on the meaning of this for practice in schools. The effect of this clarity must mean that all the members of the school—teachers, support staff and pupils—are clear about what the school stands for, what behaviour and performance are unequivocally expected from them. A key test might be that when asked all the members of the school community could give a statement of this.

EVALUATION

A feature of effective schools which is related directly to the requirement to have clear goals is the need to have a strong evaluation framework within the school. The school needs to be clear about how it is performing in terms of its goals on a regular basis. In short, effective schools are data-rich environments where there is good knowledge of current performance which is shared by all the employees.

Every goal in the school should be a SMART goal (*see* p 31) which means that it should be time-framed in the sense of specifying at what point(s) in time it should be measured to check achievement; it also means that in principle it should be measurable. Many worthwhile activities in school are difficult to measure, and what is most important in such cases is that there should be some agreement amongst the interested parties about what would constitute achievement or satisfactory performance.

Because of the complexity of many educational goals (although we would argue that there is a good deal of merit in trying to keep goals as straightforward and simple as possible), it is important that there should be a multiplicity of measures of performance in the school. For example, even for a goal like high academic achievement, schools need to go beyond conventional measures like five GCSEs A–C. Other qualifications, other test measurements, the quality of work on display, achievements of pupils outside of school might all be considered. And when it comes to goals like 'uphold the strong music traditions in the school' a variety of measures of this goal could usefully be devised.

In an age of Local Management of Schools (LMS), with a consequent heightening of interest in management matters in schools, and an increase in the sharing of management expertise between different sectors, e.g. business and education, there has been a growth in management information systems and performance data. On balance this is probably a good thing because until recently schools were hardly 'data-rich environments'. It is important to remind ourselves constantly, however, that the core business of schooling is pupil learning, and it should follow from this that the most important indicators of a school's performance should focus on teaching and learning.

Disaggregation

Of course in the age of league tables of examination and test performance schools are certainly aware of the importance of these indicators of student learning. For the league tables the data on student achievement are aggregated up to the level of the school. For the school's own purposes of determining how well it is performing this is the least helpful level because such data aggregation can hide marked data variations, particularly at the departmental level.

Schools should aim to collect data on student performance at the school level, the department level, the class level, and the individual student level. Only when this is done will there be sufficient data to determine performance, set goals and focus on under-achievement. The data at these levels should be regularly collected so that the school can build up *time series data* which will allow them to identify trends. Student performance data do tend to vary from year to year, and a three-year period is probably the safest time period on which to base any judgements at the level of the department and school.

Fine-grained data do allow one to see areas of weakness at the individual pupil level, the individual teacher level and the departmental level. These weaknesses need to be recognised so that supportive action can be taken. If the school creates a climate of fear and distrust, for either pupils or teachers, such an exercise will be very difficult, if not impossible. For data to be translated into useful management information for individual teachers or the senior management team, the school needs to have developed a climate of trust as well as a sense of purpose about the importance of student learning.

For most schools collecting their own data will not be sufficient even if they have good time series records. They will not be able to give a satisfactory answer to the question: are we performing as well as we should be? This can only be done by comparison with other schools/departments which have a similar ability/socio-economic mix. Sometimes it is possible to find a similar local school a comparison with which is reasonable, if the other school will co-operate. It is probably easier, however, to subscribe to one of the services offered by either the NFER (*see* Saunders and Schagen) or the University of Newcastle (*see* Fitz-Gibbon 1991; 1992) who will provide relevant data.

Action research

Once a school has valid and reliable data about student performance it is then in a position to improve because it will know its areas of relative weakness. However, it is one thing to know about weaknesses, and quite another thing to know how to remedy them. As our opening section on school improvement noted (*see* p 15), a dominant mode of problem-solving here is the action research strategy.

The action research model is well suited to situations where it is not wholly clear what the best course of action is. This is not uncommon in the process of school improvement when (say) the data show a mathematics department which is under-achieving, particularly with regard to the most able, but the department is surprised by the information and unclear what to do. In such circumstances one course of action is to brainstorm likely causes, or use the techniques familiar to the quality circle movement (see p 22). Such strategies are likely to provide a short list of hypotheses for the cause of the problem. Once this has been established a solution based on the most likely hypothesis needs to be implemented and carefully monitored to see if it works. In most cases there is unlikely to be any simple, straightforward solution and progress will only be made by a slow process of continual improvement.

Conclusion

In this section we have argued that once the school has set itself some goals then this must be followed up by careful and systematic data collection to check good achievement. The focus must be on collecting as much data as possible on the major goal of the school—student learning.

LEADERSHIP

It is one of the truisms of the effective schools literature to state that one of the features which distinguish effective schools is the quality of their leadership. Leadership here is to be distinguished from management. Managers are concerned to 'do things right', leaders are more concerned 'to do the right thing'. The distinguishing characteristic of an effective leader of a school is a sense of vision which is communicated to all staff and pupils.

For a long time the literature on school leadership concentrated on trying to determine the characteristic traits of effective leaders. It is possible to list those included in most of the studies. Stogdill (1974) summarises these traits as:

- sense of responsibility
- concern for task completion
- energy
- persistence
- risk-taking

- originality
- self-confidence
- capacity to handle stress
- capacity to influence
- capacity to co-ordinate the effects of others in the achievement of purpose

Although there is some merit in looking at these traits and seeing how they might be developed in school leaders, the imprecision of the language, plus the fact that some successful school leaders apparently do not exhibit all these traits all the time, casts some doubt on the utility of this approach. Furthermore, as schools have slowly begun to democratise their management, placing a greater stress on management *teams* rather than on individual leaders, it has become more common to establish to what extent the senior management team possesses the appropriate combination of qualities (Belbin, 1981).

A much more useful way of looking at the leadership of effective schools is to ask the question: what do the leaders of these schools *do*?

The most important quality of effective school leaders is a clear vision of the school that is translated into meaningful goals. As Beare, Caldwell and Millikan (1993) put it, 'outstanding leaders have a vision for their schools—a mental picture of a preferred future—which is shared with all in the school community and which shapes the programme for learning and teaching as well as policies, priorities, plans and procedures pervading the day-to-day life of the school'. So the major function of the leader is constantly to remind all the members of the school community about what the school stands for. This is achieved in various ways: by verbal exhortation, by influence over visual imagery in the school, by the use of ceremonies and rituals of the school. It is also achieved in two other important ways, however. First, by making sure that full information is available about what is going on in the school, and by making use of this information. This information can be quantitative data about achievement as well as qualitative data about behaviour. Effective heads are often described as very *visible* in the school, they engage in 'management by walking about' so that they know what is going on. Secondly, the vision of the school is reinforced by making sure that the school leaders *mirror* in their behaviour the classroom processes which they expect in their own teachers, i.e. they behave as they expect their teachers to behave in their classrooms. We might summarise this behaviour in the following way:

- high emphasis on achievement

- high expectations of performance
- strong monitoring of performance
- emphasis on the creation of an orderly atmosphere
- stress on rewards for approved behaviour rather than punishments for disapproved behaviour

Not only do the leaders of effective schools exhibit behaviour which attempts to mirror the behaviour expected of teachers in their classrooms, but effective leaders are very often involved in the core function of the school—teaching and learning. They are certainly not remote figures spending most of their time in offices far from the activity of the classroom.

One of the best ways to make sure that the school performs well and that the teachers actively share the vision of the school is to recruit teachers who are already committed to the school's vision. There are of course both difficulties and dangers here: difficulties in the sense of a shortage of certain subject teachers in some areas of the country; dangers in effectively cloning too many people with identical views so that there is no sense of challenge in the institution.

Once appropriate staff have been recruited then a prime function of school leadership is to encourage, protect and develop them. The head of the school stands at the apex of all of the school's systems; in particular he or she is the major source of incentives. Many of these rewards are symbolic (praise, clear public recognition of achievements), although some schools are developing versions of performance-related pay. Performance-related pay based on individual teacher performance is very unlikely to develop a unity of purpose in the school, and it is significant that many leading private companies have abandoned it.

Effective school studies have discovered that a satisfactory way of empowering teachers is by devolving responsibility to them. Purkey and Smith (1985) write:

> The staff of each school is given a considerable amount of responsibility and authority in determining the exact means by which they address the problem of increasing academic performance. This includes giving staff more authority over curricula and instructional decisions and allocation of building resources (p 358).

In pursuing this policy of empowerment through devolving authority the leaders of effective schools know that they must invest in the continuous development of their staff. For the leaders this means that they must spend time on the following: acting as coach, counsellor, educator, guide and champion in encouraging their staff and setting high standards. It is these sets of rules and behaviours which mark effective leaders, rather than behaviour which emphasises control, manipulation, correction, instruction and coercion

Once the leaders have devolved some responsibility to their teachers they need to capitalise on this investment. This means regarding the teachers as the core workers in the core business of the school—teaching and learning. One implication of this is that school leadership often sees that it has a key role not only in developing its teachers but in protecting them as well from unwarranted interruptions. Such a strategy can include organising in-service training on a non-disruptive basis; taking on many of the core duties themselves; protecting teachers from external disruption where appropriate.

Conclusion

We began by noting that all the effective schools literature points to the importance of school leaders. Our focus has been on trying to describe what it is that effective leaders *do* rather than in trying to identify any personality traits. We concluded that their major role was in promulgating a vision of the school that fundamentally influenced the behaviour of all the school's members.

CULTURE AND ETHOS

If one was to ask what was the single most important thing that the leaders of effective schools did, it seems reasonably clear that the answer would be given in terms of creating and maintaining an effective culture of a school. The central importance of culture is reflected in the *Ten Good Schools* report of the HMI in 1977. There they argued that:

> The schools see themselves as places designed for learning: they take the trouble to make their philosophies explicit for themselves and to explain them to parents and pupils; the foundation of their work and corporate life is an acceptance of shared values.

The HMI quotation makes reasonably clear what we mean by culture and ethos: it's about a set of shared values; values which indicate what the school stands for, what behaviour is approved and what is not. This goes beyond the goals of the school and penetrates as far as influencing the way both teachers and pupils see the world. The role of leadership is crucial here and Greenfield (1986) argues that 'leadership is a willful act where one person attempts to construct the social world for others'.

The effective school then is one with a strong and distinct culture and ethos, and gives clear messages to both staff and pupils about what is valued in the community, what sort of behaviour is encouraged or discouraged. It is different from the rules of the school in the sense that rules are exterior to people; culture and ethos are internal, shared beliefs. We can distinguish the two concepts by saying that culture refers to the values, beliefs and norms of the world of the teacher and support staff, whilst we reserve the term ethos for focusing on the world of the pupils.

An effective culture is one in which the messages about behaviour are clear and consistent and constantly point in the direction of effective teaching and learning. The elements of an effective culture usually contain the following features. First, it is a culture where pupil participation is very high. In such schools we shall find lots of offices of responsibility, lots of valued privileges; young people are given a genuine stake in the organisation of the school's space and buildings as well as in the general behaviour policy. Secondly, the adults go out of their way to create a sense of trust in the pupils. Such institutions are often marked by a strong sense of community where relations between staff and students are distinguished by friendliness and mutual respect. Thirdly, the school has an orderly, safe climate that is conducive to learning. Approved behaviour is strongly reinforced. There is a minimum of rules and regimentation but there are strong rules and sanctions on certain sorts of behaviour which are thought to be particularly detrimental to the community, for example, bullying.

From a staff perspective many effective schools are trying to develop what is known as a *learning culture*. This means not just a culture in which pupil learning is regarded as the core activity, but a culture which actively tries to monitor its own performance so that it is capable of learning how to become more effective. Two distinctive features of schools as learning organisations which are worth highlighting are: first, the sharing of information about the performance of the school throughout the staff; secondly, a distinctive way of dealing with mistakes in the school. Learning organisations seize on mistakes as opportunities to learn, the rest engage in punishments and scapegoating.

Finally, we come to the question of how the culture and ethos of a school can be constructed and maintained. These features of schools as organisations tend to develop over a longish period of time and are difficult to change. Schein (1985) argues that there are primary and secondary mechanisms for change and consolidation. The primary mechanisms are:

- what leaders pay most attention to
- how leaders react to crises and critical incidents
- role modelling, teaching and coaching by leaders
- criteria for allocating rewards and determining status
- criteria for selection, promotion and termination

The secondary mechanisms for the articulation and reinforcement of a culture are:

- the organisational culture
- systems and procedures
- space, buildings and façades
- stories and legends about important events and people
- formal statements of philosophy and policy

It is significant that Schein places formal statements of philosophy and policy last in his list. It is certainly our view that the behaviour of senior staff in the school is much more significant in determining the school's culture than formal statements of its philosophy.

SCHOOL ORGANISATION

What features of organisation might be helpful to schools in examining their present organisation and structure? The first principle is to remind oneself constantly about the core purposes of the organisation which we take to be teaching and learning. It follows from this that teachers, pupils and the sites of learning—classrooms—must be at the centre of the organisation. The management and administration of the schools are there to service its frontline core workers—teachers. If one views the school as an organisation in these terms then some features of its organisation may well look quite different. Three examples from our own experience can be used to illustrate our point. Firstly, there is the very gradual decline in posts at the deputy headteacher level as schools focus more attention on the core task of teaching and devolve management downwards. Secondly, where deputy jobs still exist a re-configuration takes place which creates posts like 'head of student/pupil services/learning' that focus attention on the core function. Finally, arrangements for teacher cover are organised in such a way that extra pressure is not placed on frontline teachers.

A more radical view of the position is what is known as the *upside-down* organisational focus (*see* Fig. 3.1)

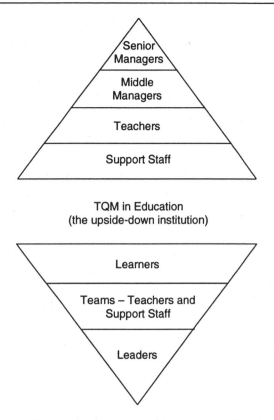

Fig. 3.1 **The hierarchical institution and the upside-down institution**

The structure emphasises the importance of the learners in the organisation and stresses also the importance of service-giving relationships.

Our second principle of effective organisation concerns the importance of *teams* in a school. We should like to focus on the importance of temporary teams and permanent school teams. When a particular issue confronts a school, like redrafting school rules or reassessing the homework policy then there seems great merit in forming a widely based team to 'solve' it. School teams invariably consist of pupils, teachers, support staff and parents, although clearly membership can and should be varied depending on the issue concerned. Such teams should be given proper facilitation support in terms of techniques of problem-solving. These *ad hoc* teams are likely to be more task-focused than standing committees, and their broad base is likely to produce better-quality decisions and a greater sense of corporate ownership.

The effective schools literature has tended to overlook the importance of the academic department as a team in the school. This is strange in view of the fact that research indicates the centrality of teaching and learning to effective schools, and it is the department which has the major responsibility for this activity. Some features of effective departments, based on our own research, are discussed on pp 47–71.

Finally, if we apply some of the findings from the literature on effective companies (see pp 23–24) and combine them with our own study of effective departments, we can appreciate the force of the Peters and Waterman dictum on tight–loose structures. Schools need to work out which features of their activities need to be heavily constrained, i.e. tightly specified and regulated, and which can be allowed to be determined on a more individual basis. Most schools will find that goals and discipline need to be tightly regulated, whereas many aspects of the teaching function (providing it is successful) should be left to an individual teacher's discretion. The balance between these elements will always be a delicate one. An analogy we have found helpful is that of the motor car. It works well when there is a good balance between engine power and steering. If it is designed so that the steering predominates (control, tightness) it goes in the right direction but with no energy; if the engine dominates (looseness) it has plenty of energy but no clear sense of direction.

Conclusion

The correlations between school effectiveness and school organisation and structure are not strong; at best we can define some broad principles of structure which we have listed as: support for frontline teachers; the importance of team working; and balance between those aspects of the organisation which need to be tightly controlled, and those which can benefit from individual energy and imagination.

PARENTAL AND COMMUNITY INVOLVEMENT

By and large effective schools are those which involve themselves closely with the local community, particularly with parents. The general reasons for this are clear enough; although children spend some 15,000 hours in schooling as pupils, this time is dwarfed by the amount of time they spend at home and in their community. It is clear that if the school and community can combine to support productive learning on the part of the pupils, then this combination has the potential to be much more powerful than the school acting alone. The difficulties obviously come if, for some reason, the culture and values of the local community are antipathetic to the potential benefits of schooling, or indifferent to it.

It is the case in Britain, as elsewhere in Europe, that parents, not schools, are primarily responsible for their child's education. Despite this fact, as Cullingford (1985) asserts,

> there has been a significant rise in the involvement of parents in schools, and many successful experiments. But even in the best examples it is clear that the mutual suspicion between parents and teachers continues. Beneath the surface of well-intended meetings lies misunderstanding and indifference.

If Cullingford is correct in his assertion, and all the evidence suggests that he is, then clearly schools have to work particularly hard to involve parents in the process of schooling. The evidence and our own experience suggest the following strategies as the ones most likely to pay dividends:

- Focus communication on pupil progress, and realise that parents are likely to be most interested in the progress of their *own* children.
- Try and bring parents inside the school as much as possible, on as many different occasions as possible. Many parents will need to be approached through 'fun' occasions in order that they may lose their suspicion of school.
- Although the traditional focus of much school–parent activity is the Parent–Teacher Association (PTA), there is some evidence to suggest that many parents find it too large, and often too full of cliques. Meetings of parents based around class and year groups are likely to be more productive.

Of course the better the records a school keeps, and the more information it collects on individual pupils the more there is to discuss with parents. This also has the advantage of keeping the school–parent relationship focused on the child and teaching and learning. Many schools treat parents and the PTA as fund-raisers and cheap labour for routine tasks. Such a focus is unlikely to produce effective schooling.

In recent years the idea of school–parent contracts has attracted much interest. It is based on the idea that the relationship might usefully be seen as requiring reciprocal obligations. Macbeth (1993) argues that 'in exchange for taking a child into school (relieving parents of the technical burden of education minimally), parents would be asked to sign an understanding that they have obligations related to that schooling process' (p 198). The suggested contract is reproduced in Fig. 3.2.

I, being the parent/guardian of . . . .(name of child)
acknowledge that **I understand**:
(1) that prime responsibility for my child's education rests with me by law;
(2) that the school will assist me to carry out that responsibility;
(3) that my active support for my child's schooling may increase his/her likelihood of gaining maximum benefit from it.

Further, **I undertake** to do the following to the best of my ability:
(a) to attend private consultations with my child's teacher(s) at mutually convenient times;
(b) to read written reports sent by the school and to respond to them;
(c) to attend class meetings or other meetings arranged to explain the curriculum and the ways in which it can be reinforced at home;
(d) to provide suitable conditions and support for my child's homework;
(e) to provide such information as the school shall require for educational purposes;
(f) to support school rules;
(g) to abide by decisions made by the headteacher and the governing body with regard to the school's management.

Signature of parent/guardian . . . .   Date . . . .

Fig. 3.2 Draft school–parent contract

Source: Macbeth (1993)

This completes our review of the major features of effective schools. We must repeat our view that such lists of characteristics should not be seen as some sort of recipe to be adopted by other schools. Rather, it could more usefully form an agenda which might be discussed with key school constituencies, particularly with the teaching staff. Each school is unique, with its own particular blend of staff, pupils and parents, and each must find its own model of effectiveness. Other people's models are useful because they lend a sense of perspective to internal deliberations which can become too inward-looking. It is appropriate therefore for us to end this section by reproducing two of the best-known models of school effectiveness. The first is the 'Halton' model, developed among a group of secondary schools in Ontario, Canada. Fig. 3.3 summarises its major features.

The other model is drawn from one of the best-known studies of school effectiveness in the UK, the ILEA Junior school study by Peter Mortimore and his colleagues. The twelve key features of effective junior schools are reproduced below as Fig. 3.4.

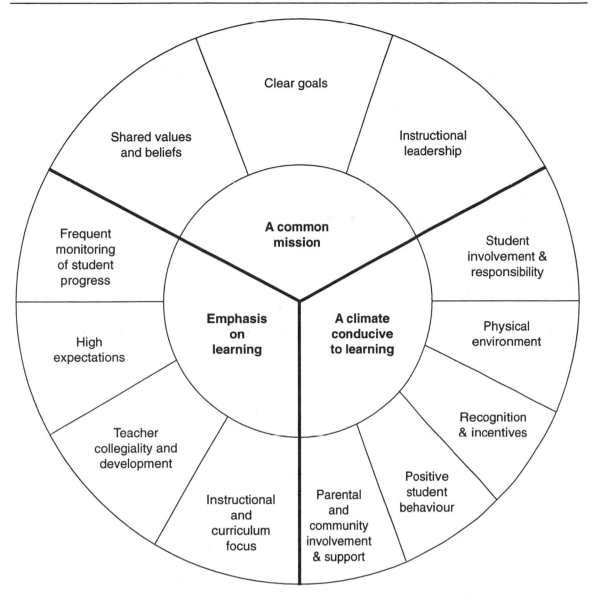

Fig. 3.3 Characteristics of effective schools (the 'Halton' model)

(1) Purposeful leadership of the staff by the headteacher;

(2) The involvement of the deputy head;

(3) The involvement of teachers;

(4) Consistency amongst teachers;

(5) Structured sessions;

(6) Intellectually challenging teaching;

(7) The work-centred environment;

(8) Limited focus within sessions;

(9) Maximum communication between teachers and pupils;

(10) Record-keeping;

(11) Parental involvement;

(12) Positive climate.

Fig. 3.4 Twelve key factors of school effectiveness taken from the ILEA Junior School Study

Source: Mortimore *et al.* (1988)

PART TWO

INTRODUCTION

The main purpose of Part Two is to move from the *macro* level of whole school effectiveness and improvement, to the *micro* level of classroom effectiveness and improvement. The 'Halton' model as outlined in Part One (Fig. 3.3), described a 'nested' model approach to school improvement which operated at a number of levels (Stoll and Fink, 1992). In the 'Halton' model, it was argued that for 'real' improvement to take place, change needed to occur at the level of the whole school, at departmental or faculty level, and at the level of the classroom. Fullan (1988) refers to this as *the sub-processes of change*, with its many routes and layers within an organisation.

As demonstrated in Part One, research on effective schooling in secondary schools has identified generic characteristics and processes associated with effective schooling and school improvement. It has however, stopped short of articulating and explaining the *sub-processes* of institutional improvement. The purpose of Part Two therefore, is to consider *sub-processes* of improvement within the context of the classroom.

The effective classroom as conceptualised in Part Two has three dimensions. The first is an organisational dimension which involves a consideration of departmental or faculty effectiveness. The second is the pedagogical dimension which incorporates effective teaching and learning. The third dimension is the managerial dimension which involves the process and practice of managing effective teaching and learning. Part Two, starts by looking at the organisational dimension of the effective classroom and considers what constitutes departmental, or faculty effectiveness.

Departmental/faculty effectiveness

INTRODUCTION

Research into effective departments has revealed that there are features or characteristics which effective departments or faculties consistently display (*see* Fitz-Gibbon, 1991, 1992; Harris *et al*, 1995). While the complexity and uniqueness of each school context is acknowledged, there are some generic features of effective departments or faculties which will be outlined in this section. Initially, the relationship between whole-school management and effective departments will be discussed.

Many research studies have shown that the style of management adopted within a school is centrally important in the perceived and realised effectiveness of the whole school (DFE, 1993). As noted earlier, it is a commonplace observation in the effective schooling literature to suggest that for departments to be really effective they need to be 'nested' inside schools which are themselves managed effectively. The 'Halton' model has particularly endorsed this viewpoint (Stoll and Fink, 1992).

Recent research has found that there are several aspects of whole-school policy which effective departments build upon (Sammons *et al*, 1995; Harris *et al*, 1995). The first of these is the emphasis placed upon pupils. This usually goes far beyond the usual professional rhetoric. Effective schools, like effective departments, place pupil learning and well-being at the very centre of their work. Similarly, effective departments tend to be located in schools which are centrally concerned with providing a caring environment for pupils. These schools are characterised by the emphasis placed upon involving pupils fully in the life of the school. Effective schools tend to be overtly concerned with raising the expectations of both pupils *and* staff. Research findings have shown the importance of raising pupils expectations in the search for increased effectiveness (e.g. Mortimore *et al*, 1988).

The second aspect of whole-school policy which has been found to have an impact at departmental level is an emphasis upon pupils' behaviour and rewards. Schools which have policies emphasising the importance of rewarding positive behaviour and which acknowledge a wide range of achievements (not just academic) are more likely to be effective. Using rewards rather than punishments to change behaviour within departments is an important factor in raising pupil motivation. Additionally, the use of merits or rewards to signify pupil success is found to be more effective if used consistently within, and across departments (*see* case study B).

Recent research has shown that there are common features which effective departments consistently display.

A CLIMATE FOR IMPROVEMENT

Within effective departments there frequently exists a *climate for change* or *a climate for improvement*. This is a climate in which the department is committed to improvement and is prepared to change existing practices. Developing this climate has been found to be a necessary pre-requisite of departmental change. For example, increased collegiate modes of working within departments, or a change of Head of Department (HoD), can create such a *climate for improvement*. Without this climate, research has shown that departments will continue to modify, rather than change, existing practices (Harris *et al*, 1995).

VISION

Effective departments, like effective schools, can be identified by their clear and shared sense of vision. This vision shapes the Head of Department's management style, influences the departmental view of the subject and affects the organisation of teaching and learning within the department. One of the most striking findings from the various research studies into departmental effectiveness has been the collegiate vision adopted by effective departments. Effective departments tend to be *talking departments*, i.e. departments that are marked by a constant interchange of professional information at both formal and informal levels. Within effective departments meetings are frequent and all departmental members are usually involved in the shaping of policy.

COLLEGIALITY

Within effective departments research has shown that there is an emphasis on collegiality and co-operation. This also extends to the style of management adopted by the Head of Department. The management style which has been found to be most characteristic of effective departments is that of the *leading professional*. Here the Head of Department's own professional practice is regarded by other departmental members as the model to follow, particularly in teaching. In short, effective departments operate collegiately to improve their teaching and they tend to achieve this goal by basing their practice on the highest professional standards.

ORGANISATION AND RESOURCE MANAGEMENT

In managerial terms, effective departments are those that possess the ability to organise key elements of teaching and learning in the optimum way. Effective departments tend to be highly organised and generate detailed and collectively agreed schemes of work. Research has shown that the schemes of work within effective departments display certain characteristics:

- they reflect the departmental vision of 'good' practice in teaching and learning
- they are very detailed and offer clear guidance on teaching approaches
- they are regarded as important documents by departmental members and are easily accessible to all within the department
- they are collectively produced and agreed

In order to translate these schemes of work into effective teaching and learning strategies, the management of resources is evidently very important. It has been shown that effective departments tend to manage their resources to the advantage of the whole department and to the advantage of all pupils. For example, one research project describes how a science department decided to buy enough sets of basic equipment so that *all* pupils in that department could carry out the majority of experiments. In this way the department did not disadvantage any pupil, or groups of pupils (Harris *et al*, 1994). In short, the research found that for most effective departments the *bottom line* was the enhancement of teaching and learning for *all* pupils, and that this was achieved through the optimum allocation of resources.

MONITORING AND EVALUATION

Within effective schools monitoring and evaluation have been shown to be important dual processes. The latter has been found to be particularly important for departmental planning (English and Harris, 1992). In effective departments, the mechanisms for monitoring pupil progress have been found to be tightly in place. Information about the progress of individual students is usually systematically collected through a variety of means and is shared within and across departments/faculties. In addition, effective departments keep detailed profiles of pupils to chart individual progress. These profiles often include detailed assessments of pupils' strengths and weaknesses in the subject area and are regularly shared with pupils.

Effective departments have been shown to be departments which *self-evaluate*. They are mostly departments which place a high premium on both the process and outcomes of self-evaluation. Research has shown that effective departments know their own strengths and weaknesses and collect systematic evidence of their progress towards set departmental goals.

EFFECTIVE TEACHING AND LEARNING

At the heart of any effective department is the effective organisation of teaching and learning. While both effective teaching and learning will be dealt with later in this book, it is worth considering these aspects in direct relation to departmental effectiveness. It is clear from the research findings that effective departments have certain set protocols in relation to teaching and learning. For example, the opportunity to offer pupils regular feedback on their progress is central to the work of these departments.

Similarly, effective departments take a great deal of time and effort to select *what* to teach their pupils. Effective departments find content and ways of teaching it which match the capacities and interests of their pupils. Also, effective departments take care to translate the selected syllabus into carefully crafted schemes of work.

Effective departments are also characterised by the care and attention which they pay to the process of *assessment*. The assessment systems of effective departments include the following features:

- detailed and up-to-date record keeping, e.g a sophisticated spreadsheet of student marks
- emphasis is placed upon trying to make marking *consistent* within the department
- efforts are made to try and give the pupils, particularly the older ones, a stake in the assessment, e.g. pupils are often invited to comment on

each other's and their own work. Pupils are encouraged to discuss their marks with the teacher in order to try and understand the strengths and weaknesses of their own efforts

- using the assessment system as the vehicle for frequent feedback to the pupils. Feedback tends to be more criterion-referenced than norm-referenced

These features of assessment have been found to provide pupils with a clear sense of progression which promotes and assists individual motivation.

To sum up, effective teaching and learning within departments is stimulated and strengthened when:

- there is an attempt to involve all pupils in the learning process by providing a variety of tasks which deal with individual, small-group, and large-group situations
- teachers encourage co-operative learning where pupils work together as part of a team-sharing experience, being given different roles and developing their own self esteem
- pupils are actively involved in a review and consideration of the learning process and
- teachers develop meaningful, formative and motivational forms of assessment which reinforce and build confidence.

CONCLUSION

From this analysis of effective departments a number of key features emerge. Firstly, it would appear that effective departments enjoy a collegiate management style and share a strong vision of their subject. Secondly, effective departments are well organised in terms of assessment, record-keeping, homework, etc, and employ good resource management. Thirdly, effective departments have efficient systems for monitoring and evaluating pupil progress which enables them to provide structured and regular feedback. Fourthly, effective departments operate very clear routines and practices within lessons. Finally, effective departments have a strong pupil-centred ethos that systematically rewards pupils and provides every opportunity for autonomous pupil learning. In short, effective departments are centrally concerned with *effective teaching*.

The next section will consider the processes and practice of effective teaching in some detail.

Effective teaching

INTRODUCTION

This section focuses on effective teaching. The term 'effective teaching' is used here in a much broader sense than simply teaching behaviour. While teaching behaviour is acknowledged to be important, this section focuses upon the underlying processes and practice of effective teaching. It considers the managerial and organisational aspects of effective teaching, as well as the pedagogical influences.

The section concentrates upon the factors at classroom level which lead to effective teaching. As stated in Part One, factors at whole-school level influence education at the classroom level, in the same way that the societal context of education influences education both generally and locally. Learning at the classroom level therefore takes place within a unique school context, which will shape and influence the way in which effective teaching is construed and enacted. Consequently, in outlining the features of effective teaching, it is recognised that they will vary depending on the particular school context and environment.

In considering educational activity at the classroom level, teacher activities can be divided into *management* and *teaching* behaviour. This distinction can be described as follows:

- *Management* refers to everything teachers do to *organise* their classroom in order to make teaching possible.
- *Teaching behaviour* incorporates only *teaching activities* which include different teaching strategies, or styles.

In this section, the generic features of effective teaching are considered, which include both management and teaching behaviour. To begin with, however, the general issues surrounding effective teaching are discussed.

EFFECTIVE TEACHING

Much of the debate about effective teaching revolves around the issue of providing equal and sufficient *opportunities to learn* for all children in all schools. Clearly, providing equal and improved opportunities to learn should be at the heart of all efforts to improve both the quality and equality in education. However, as Woods (1990) notes, opportunities to learn also require *opportunities to teach*. The argument for providing teachers with sufficient *opportunities to teach* seems persuasive enough but what exactly does this mean in practice?

Hargreaves and Fullan (1992) offer three interpretations of *opportunities to teach* which revolve around the central notion of effective teaching. These interpretations are as follows:

- First, opportunities to teach mean having sufficient opportunities to learn and acquire the knowledge and skills of effective teaching;
- secondly, opportunities to teach entail having opportunities to develop personal qualities, commitment and self-understanding essential to becoming a sensitive and flexible teacher;
- thirdly, opportunities to teach necessitate creating a work environment which is supportive and not restrictive of professional learning and continuous improvement, i.e. an environment where the emphasis is placed upon effective teaching and where resources are allocated upon this basis.

It is evident from the previous section which examined effective departments that all three interpretations are important if teachers are to become more effective. Another obvious way of enabling teachers to become *more effective* is to equip them with more knowledge about the different learning styles of their pupils. Research has shown that teachers who are more skilled and flexible in their teaching strategies and more knowledgeable about their subject matter, are more likely to be more effective and to improve the achievement levels of their pupils.

Scheerens (1992) has argued that of all the charactereristics of school effectiveness it is those that relate to teaching that have been proved most relevant. Research has shown that teaching approaches, if carefully selected, can influence a range of outcomes in both the cognitive and the affective domains (Mortimore *et al*, 1988). Consequently, it would seem important to consider what is known about the effectiveness of different teaching approaches or teaching styles.

Effective teaching styles

Unlike learning, teaching is an overt activity and should therefore be easier to describe and evaluate. There have been numerous theories of teaching approaches, or styles, but the effective teacher does not necessarily fit neatly into such categories, or typologies. Effective teachers adopt various teaching styles which can range between extreme opposites.

In his study of teaching styles and pupil progress, Bennett (1976) used the polarised terms *progressive* and *traditional* teaching to describe opposite ends of a teaching-style continuum. From a theoretical review of the literature and from a series of interviews with head and class teachers from twelve schools the characteristics of *progressive* and *traditional* teachers were considered by Bennett to be as follows:

Progressive	Traditional
1 Integrated subject matter	1 Separate subject matter
2 Teacher as guide to educational experiences	2 Teacher as distributor of knowledge
3 Active pupil role	3 Passive pupil role
4 Pupils participate in curriculum planning	4 Pupils have no say in curriculum planning
5 Learning predominantly by discovery techniques	5 Accent on memory, practice and rote
6 External rewards and punishments not necessary, i.e. intrinsic motivation	6 External rewards used, e.g. grades, i.e. extrinsic motivation
7 Not too concerned with conventional academic standards	7 Concerned with academic standards
8 Little testing	8 Regular testing
9 Accent on co-operative group work	9 Accent on competition
10 Teaching not confined to classroom base	10 Teaching confined to classroom base
11 Accent on creative expression	11 Little emphasis on creative expression

Source: Bennett (1976) p 38

Brandes and Ginnis (1986) later supplemented Bennett's typology with the following two additional statements.

Progressive	Traditional
12 Cognitive and affective domains given equal emphasis	12 Cognitive domain is emphasised
13 Process is valued	13 Little attention is paid to process

Source: Brandes and Ginnis (1986)

Both research studies emphasised the fact that while the two typologies were at opposite ends of the continuum, they were not the only two styles available. Research findings consistently show that teachers engage in different teaching styles for different contexts, not necessarily always at one end of the continuum or the other (Creemers, 1994; Kyriacou, 1986).

In the traditional approach, it was suggested that the teacher was responsible for the task of interpreting the needs of every individual pupil in the group. The model was one of the teacher instructing and instilling pre-determined skills and knowledge in the pupil. The teacher controlled events and the pupils were totally dependent on him/her to learn. Brandes and Ginnis (1986) suggested that the problem with this approach was that it did not educate pupils to take responsibility for their own learning, to be self-evaluating and self-determining. They were expected to learn by *example* and not by *discovery*.

In the contrasting progressive approach, it was suggested that pupils were mainly responsible for their own learning. In this approach, the teacher became more of a 'facilitator' of learning rather than directing the learning by taking a central instructional role. Initiatives like Technical and Vocational Education Initiative (TVEI) termed this approach as 'flexible' or 'negotiated learning' and research in this area revealed that teachers involved in TVEI were moving towards 'facilitating' this end of the continuum.

Whatever the relative merits of different teaching approaches or styles there is little concrete evidence in favour of one approach rather than another (Bennett, 1976; Mortimore *et al*, 1988). In terms of enhancing teacher effectiveness in the classroom, it would appear that a mixture of approaches or methods is preferable. Indeed the research on teacher effectiveness is still relatively consistent in emphasising the importance of having a repertoire of different teaching approaches (Creemers, 1994; Kyriacou, 1986).

Teacher effectiveness

Over the past two decades, research into teacher effectiveness has made a significant contribution to the wider educational debate on school effectiveness. Teachers' behaviour in the classroom is one aspect of school effectiveness which impinges directly on the experiences and thus the attainments of pupils. Several authors have highlighted the difficulty of establishing a direct link between particular aspects of school effectiveness and students' learning (Coker *et al*, 1988; Mortimore and MacBeath, 1994).In particular, Kyriacou (1986) has outlined the shortcomings of process–product studies of teacher effectiveness.

A major problem in studing teacher effectiveness is the diversity of teaching situations and contexts. Some studies have attempted to get round this problem by exploring more subject-specific contexts, such as science (Eggleston *et al*, 1976) or mathematics (Heene and Schulsman, 1988). Even then, the relationship between 'a particular' teaching approach and student learning outcomes is not clear-cut.

Emerging from this work, other research on effective teaching has focused either some aspect of pupil behaviour as the criterion for effectiveness, or the perceptions of those involved in the lesson as a mechanism for judging teacher effectiveness. In one recent research project teachers attempted to relate the effectiveness of different learning and teaching initiatives to the development of a number of transferable skills (Devine *et al*, 1994). The majority of teachers involved believed that flexible learning (as defined by the school) influenced positively the development of oral communication, encouraging students to work individually, solve problems on their own and take responsibility. They reported noticing an improvement in students' skills in these areas.

The most extensive work on models of teaching has been carried out by Joyce and Showers (1991). They defined a number of models of teaching designed to bring about particular kinds of learning. They argued that teachers should be able to identify these models and to select the ones that they should master, to increase their teaching competence.

Despite the difficulties identified above, there is a degree of consensus about the generic features or components of effective teaching (Bennett, 1991; Bickel and Bickel, 1986; Brophy, 1983; Rosenshine, 1983; Walberg, 1990; Wang, 1991). While there are differences of emphasis and detail between findings, there is consistency across the research studies. A useful synthesis of these findings of this research is provided by Porter and Brophy (1988). They suggest a view of effective teachers as semi-autonomous professionals who possess certain attributes or features.

Effective teachers

- are clear about their teaching goals

- are knowledgeable about the content of their subject and the strategies for teaching it

- are able to communicate to their pupils what is expected of them and why

- make expert use of existing teaching materials in order to devote more time to practices that enrich and clarify the content

- are knowledgeable about their pupils, adapting teaching to their needs and anticipating misconceptions in their existing knowledge

- teach pupils metacognitive strategies and give them opportunities to master them

- address higher, as well as, lower cognitive objectives

- monitor pupils' understanding by offering regular, appropriate feedback

- integrate their teaching with that in other subject areas

- accept responsibility for pupils' results

- are thoughtful and reflective about their practice

Source: Porter and Brophy (1988)

The literature on effective teaching is replete with the cues and tactics necessary for effective teaching. For example, Doyle (1987 p 95) outlines how pupils can achieve more through certain sets of teacher behaviour.

Pupils achieve more when a teacher:

- emphasises academic goals

- makes academic goals explicit and expects pupils to be able to master the curriculum

- carefully organises and sequences the curriculum

- clearly explains and illustrates what pupils are to learn

- frequently asks direct and specific questions to monitor students' progress and check their understanding

- provides pupils with ample opportunity to practise

- gives prompt feedback to ensure success

- corrects mistakes and allows pupils to use a skill until it is over-learned or automatic

- reviews regularly and holds pupils accountable for work

Source: Doyle (1987)

From this perspective, a teacher promotes pupil learning by being active in planning and organising his or her teaching effectively.

The following sub-section considers the practical *components* of effective teaching.

THE COMPONENTS OF EFFECTIVE TEACHING

Planning

Good planning is acknowledged to be a crucial component of effective teaching. Planning is linked to the notion of *preparedness* where a lesson is viewed by pupils as being well organised, with a coherent structure. Additionally, such lessons contain a sense of purposefulness for both the teacher and the pupils. In essence, an effective lesson is one in which the teacher knows exactly what he or she wants to achieve and relays this with confidence and enthusiasm to pupils. It is a lesson which has clearly identified pupil learning outcomes which are shared with pupils.

Experienced teachers have a store of wisdom concerning the components of effective lessons, which enables them to spend much less time planning than is the case for inexperienced teachers. However, the elements of planning a lesson are the same for all teachers, whether novice or expert:

- The aims need to be carefully considered and the objectives for the lesson clearly set out;
- The context of the lesson must be considered, as well as the type of pupils, the room layout, the time of day, and an effective learning environment should be prepared by the teacher taking into consideration all these components;
- There is need to monitor and evaluate pupils' educational progress through the process of review target setting to enable the teacher to judge whether the lesson has been effective or not.

These are questions which teachers should ask themselves to assist their planning.

Effective lesson planning and presentation

- Does the lesson cater appropriately for the level and range of ability in the class?
- What do pupils already know about the subject/topic?
- What do I want pupils to learn in this lesson? How will this relate to past learning and to the course of study as a whole?
- What resources do I have to hand? How shall I use them to best effect?
- What teaching methods/styles shall I adopt? How will this suit the topic/pupils in question?
- What preparation is needed directly before the lesson? What teaching materials/resources shall I need?
- What assessment procedures shall I use during/following the lesson?
- How shall I evaluate my own performance and that of the lesson as a whole?

A particular part of planning which assists effective teaching in action is that of *advanced mapping*. This refers to the way in which a teacher indicates at the start of the lesson how the content and learning activities of the lesson will be organised, and are related to the pupils' previous knowledge and understanding. In other words the format and purpose of the lesson is made explicit to the pupils.

Recent research into effective departments, outlined in the previous section, demonstrated that teachers in effective departments were good at making effective maps to guide pupil learning (Jamieson, Russ, and Harris, 1994). An essential part of effective teaching has been shown to be the skill of considering what sense the learner will make of the lesson; also, more importantly, how pupils can be helped in making connections between various learning experiences (Driver, 1983).

A simple verbal or written map from the teacher at the start of every lesson to assist pupils in making such cognitive connections will orientate pupils towards effective learning. Guidance from the teacher which contextualises learning for pupils is time well spent. It helps pupils to know where they are in their learning and where they will be going next. It is also more likely to lead to meaningful teaching and meaningful learning.

Meaningful learning

Meaningful teaching and *meaningful learning* are ideas grounded in the approaches to teaching and learning outlined by Gagne (1985), Ausubel (1968) and Bruner (1960). Essentially, these approaches stress that sophisticated information processing must be undertaken by the learner for learning to take place. There are *three* main stages in the model of meaningful learning.

1 The first stage is concerned with the *initial reception* of sensory information. This involves taking account of the learner's level of attention and the degree to which such attention is directed towards aspects of the whole range of sensory inputs available in the classroom. At the same time, initial reception is also subject to *selective perception*, which acts as a filter and alerts the learner to the most significant aspects of the sensory information available. This information processing lasts only seconds but involves attention and selective perception.
2 The second stage occurs when information is *processed* through the short-term memory and involves the *application* of cognitive processes.
3 In the third stage *cognitive restructuring* allows learning to be held in the long-term memory.

Effective learning requires *all three stages* to be completed.

In rote learning, unlike meaningful learning, what is learned is characterised by arbitrary associations with the learner's previous knowledge. Rarely are the connections made explicit or visible for the learner. Meaningful learning therefore has important implications for the notion of teaching for understanding, since it places emphasis on the changes in the pupil's cognitive structure that take place during learning, and the consequent demonstration of learning that the learner can display (Kyriacou,1986).

Meaningful learning takes place when:

- The teacher makes explicit the connections between areas of knowledge for the pupil
- The teacher allows time for pupils to express their ideas and to expand on them
- The teacher encourages abstract thought and analysis of ideas
- The teacher encourages a testing of ideas and a transfer of concepts to gain understanding
- The pupils feel able to criticise information and ideas in a constructive manner
- The pupils seek to structure their knowledge in a meaningful and accessible way
- The pupils are not afraid to express value judgements and to have them discussed

---

Inter-personal climate

For meaningful learning to take place, connections have to be made explicit for the learner and the inter-personal climate in the classroom has to be suitable. The inter-personal climate refers to the communication between teachers and pupils in the classroom. If effective teaching is to take place then the teacher needs to consider how he or she might provide the optimum inter-personal climate within the classroom.

Inter-personal climate

- The teacher shows a personal interest in individual pupils for their own sake beyond the needs of the immediate task
- The teacher actively fosters a sense of group cohesion in work and in discipline
- The teacher is courteous and frequently accepts a pupil's expression of feeling about the work or the organisation
- The teacher makes frequent use of praise and encouragement but in a measured and sensitive way
- The teacher and pupils share their sense of humour

Source: Waterhouse (1990)

Cognitive matching

The work of Piaget (1972) in studying the cognitive development of children has had a significant impact upon discussions surrounding effective teaching and learning in schools. In particular, his focus on the processes of assimilation and accommodation in characterising different stages of children's thinking and learning is well known. The importance of his work when considering effective teaching lies in his identification of a child's knowledge and cognitive processes at a given time. In other words, his work highlights the importance of matching content or knowledge to a child's stage of intellectual development.

This principle of *cognitive matching* is an important one for effective teaching and learning. The need to pitch the learning experience at the right level for each child is important for two reasons. First, because the learning experience has to promote an experience from which the child can make links or associations. It needs to be an experience that connects other past learning experiences to enable the child to extend knowledge and understanding (*see* Driver, 1983; Claxton, 1990). The importance of explicit connections in learning has already been mentioned and is the basis upon which learners can assimilate and accommodate learning. Without this conceptual mapping, effective learning is less likely to occur.

Secondly, Piaget (1972) argued that the notion of readiness is important for effective learning to take place. He suggested that pupils must be ready to learn in both motivational and cognitive development terms. The notion of readiness does not mean that teachers should wait passively until pupils reach a particular observable state but rather that teachers should contribute to appropriate learning activities at appropriate times.

The appropriate matching of content to the stage of a child's development is also more likely to prompt *transfer of learning*. Transfer of learning refers to a pupil's ability to make use of previous learning in dealing with new tasks and situations. It is the teacher's role to facilitate the transfer of learning by mapping out the learning for learners. By carefully matching content to the learner and to previous learning, effective transfer can take place. If there is an absence of connection between the two processes of learning, learners will be more likely to compartmentalise learning and to create barriers between different learning experiences.

The failure to retrieve information is also a function of inappropriate or inadequate connections being in place in the learner's mind. The subject-based curriculum does little to break down the barriers created between knowledge and can lead to compartmentalisation of learning. Therefore, teachers need to give pupils practice in transferring knowledge and making connections across subject areas.

Cognitive matching

- Content is carefully matched to the stage of intellectual development in the learner
- Content is carefully matched to the learning needs of individual learners
- Content is matched to previous content, and connections are made explicit
- Content is transferred from other subject areas and the transfer of knowledge is rehearsed among learners
- Content is not delivered in a compartmentalised way

Translation

Effective teaching is essentially the translation of complex information, concepts and knowledge for learners. Researchers have noted that in some cases, problems of understanding subject matter are common to pupils being taught by both apparently effective teachers and less effective teachers. Such studies have reinforced the view that barriers to effective learning may lie in the subject matter itself rather than in general qualities of the teaching or learning activities in which learners are engaged.

The subject complexities of science or history may require careful translation for pupils for learning to take place. The subject's *taken for granted* phrases or terminology might require careful translation if learners are to get to grips with complex phenomena or concepts. For example, some teachers have encouraged learners to use a vocabulary book full of the learners' own explanations for concepts or terminology as a useful and practical aid to learning (*see* case study A below). Similarly, other teachers have prepared the translation of their subject by offering learners accessible ways into the subject through summary sheets explaining terminology.

This breaking up of subject content into meaningful parts for the learners is another feature of effective learning. The chunking up of subject content gives learners access to the subject in selected stages which avoids overload and reduces the potential for retrieval failure.

Teachers might need to consider the following questions:

> **Translation**
>
> - Is my subject accessible to learners?
> - Have I translated key subject terminology adequately?
> - Have I encouraged learners to translate the subject into their own vocabulary?
> - Is there a common understanding of the concepts?
> - Is the subject divided into appropriately sized chunks for learners?
> - Could I help in translating exam or test questions into more meaningful questions for learners?

Effective teaching time

The research literature has consistently shown that active teaching time is an important construct of effective learning (Anderson, 1984; Corno, 1979; Creemers,1994). This refers to the time learners spend being actively engaged in the learning task and in activities designed to bring about the desired educational outcomes. Early research concentrated on the amount of time learners spent on outcome-related tasks, and indicated that the more time spent 'on task' the greater are the gains in educational attainment.

Such studies often demonstrated how learning time was wasted during an ineffective lesson, most often on discipline, or on issues related to classroom management. In such lessons it was found that learners were not 'on task' for the greater part of their classroom time. More recent studies have tried to move away from the proportion of time formula which was acknowledged to be overly simplistic. Instead of noting the amount of time learners spent on an activity, the time spent *actively engaged* in that activity is now considered to be of paramount importance to effective teaching.

Research has shown that the achievement of learners is heavily influenced by the way time is allocated by teachers and used by learners in classrooms (Kyriacou, 1986). It follows that interventions which affect instructional time or active learning time will affect achievement. Yet time alone is not the measure of quality in teaching. In thinking about academic learning time it is necessary to consider not only whether pupils are paying attention, but also what they are doing, e.g. solving work problems, answering questions or writing essays. In other words, not only is the amount of time pupils spend 'on task' essential for effective teaching but also, the nature of the task is important for effective learning to take place.

> **Effective teaching time**
>
> - The teacher succeeds in allocating a high proportion of the available time to academic work
> - The learners spend a high proportion of their time engaged on their learning tasks
> - The learners experience a high degree of success during their active learning time
> - The teacher maintains a good balance in the use of time, organisational, managerial, etc
> - A high proportion of the teacher's time is spent in substantive interaction with the learners, e.g. questioning, explaining, describing
> - Simple and speedy procedures have been devised for tackling routine events and repeated problems
> - The teacher regularly reviews the lesson in terms of the effective use of time by both teacher and pupils

Quality of teaching

A number of writers have attempted to identify the key aspects of high-quality teaching or instruction (Haertel *et al*, 1983) and have focused upon the psychological aspects of instruction such as the effects of reinforcement on learning. Other writers on this theme have focused upon general qualities (or teaching skills) which seem to be of importance such as cognitive matching and pacing mentioned earlier.

Classroom studies of teaching effects, however, have generally supported a direct and structured approach to teaching. That is, pupils usually achieve more when a teacher follows certain *teaching quality* rules (see following box).

From this perspective a teacher promotes learning by being active in planning and organising instruction, explaining to pupils what they are to learn, arranging occasions for guided practice, monitoring progress, providing feedback, and otherwise helping pupils to understand and accomplish work. In this role the teacher is the leader and presenter of learning and demonstrates personal attributes, technical competencies and subject knowledge that will promote pupil's learning in an atmosphere of respect and confidence.

> **Quality teaching**
>
> involves creating a learning environment which:
>
> - emphasises learning goals and makes them explicit
> - outlines learning purposes and potential learning outcomes
> - carefully organises and sequences curriculum experiences
> - explains and illustrates what pupils are to learn
> - frequently asks direct and specific questions to monitor students' progress and check their understanding
> - provides pupils with ample opportunity to practise, gives prompt feedback to ensure success and corrects errors
> - reviews regularly and holds pupils accountable for work

Teacher and learner expectations

An important part of effective teaching is the extent to which learners feel that they are expected to learn and how this expectation of learning is reinforced. Research on learning theory stresses the importance of individual differences amongst learners and underlines the need for learners to believe in themselves as learners. A relatively new strand of work on learning theory concerns what is known as *self-efficacy* (Wood and Bandura, 1989). In this theory the learners' beliefs in themselves are reinforced or reduced and the effects on achievement noted. The research shows that the stronger their feeling of self-efficacy the better the level of achievement. Moreover, the individual's feeling is influenced by the school attended. If teachers hold positive views about ability and about their teaching skills they are more likely to produce academic learning in their classrooms.

Essentially, these research findings demonstrate the importance of teacher expectations for their pupils' learning. Where teachers hold high expectations of pupils' ability their pupils are more likely to achieve. Yet it has been shown that teachers in certain socio-economic contexts consistently exhibit low expectations of pupils' ability.

Similarly, attribution theory illuminates how learners understand and react to their achievements. Research has shown that achievement can be judged by learners in either internal or external ways. If achievement is judged by learners in terms of internal factors such as lack of ability or lack of effort the result is demotivation and a reluctance to learn. Alternatively, if achievement is judged in external ways such as poor teaching or scarcity of books, the effect on motivation is less damaging. In this case failure is ascribed to external factors and does not damage a pupil's motivation to learn because it is viewed as not *their fault*.

Dweck and Repucci (1973) argue that girls and boys attribute failure to quite different causes: girls to lack of ability (internal) and boys to their lack of effort (internal) or bad luck (external) and that their teachers, often unwittingly, provide differential feedback to boys and girls. The net result of this is that learners are less likely to do well if the reinforcement obtained from the teacher focuses on internal causes. To increase motivation teachers need to move away from internal causes and to raise expectations through focusing on positive achievement and learning gain. To summarise:

Teacher expectations of pupil learning:

- influences pupil motivation towards learning
- affects pupils' belief in their capacity to learn
- can reinforce negative opinions about pupils' capacity to learn
- can raise pupil learning performance
- can alter pupils' expectation

Pupils' expectations about their learning:

- are derived from teachers' feedback
- can influence their motivation to learn
- can add to internal causation of lack of achievement
- can be altered

Teacher expectations are clearly linked to motivation for learning and achievement and are therefore important for effective teaching to take place.

Motivation

Teacher expectations have been shown to be highly influential in motivating pupil learning but there are other important considerations regarding motivation. *Intrinsic motivation* involves an interest in the learning task itself and also satisfaction gained from the task. Intrinsic motivation has been elaborated in a number of ways. White (1959) has argued that individuals have a basic drive towards competence as well as curiosity. He also argues that individuals have a drive towards joining in with others in order to achieve some objectives. Learning by participating or co-operative learning are ways in which this can be achieved in the classroom.

Extrinsic motivation, on the other hand, refers to those learning situations where the impetus for the motivation stems from satisfying a personal drive. In this case, the learning task is seen to be a means towards an end which may be in part contingent on the successful completion of the task but is not derived from the task itself. The view of seeing motivation as deriving from an attempt to satisfy one's needs is particularly pertinent when thinking about pupil learning. It has been suggested that teachers can affect pupils' extrinsic motivation quite considerably.

The literature on school effectiveness and school improvement has consistently shown the importance of the immediate environment on learning and pupils' motivation to learn (*see* Rutter *et al*, 1979; Mortimore *et al*, 1988). In particular, these research studies have highlighted how the environment of the school, and in particular the classroom, is especially influential for pupil learning.

The environment of the classroom

- Is the room clean and tidy, occupied only by equipment and materials in use?
- Are wall displays attractively arranged and relevant to current teaching and learning?
- Are relevant reading and reference materials available to pupils at all times, without the need to request them?
- Does the layout of furniture give pupils as much work space as possible?
- Is there an adequate supply of all the writing and drawing materials and equipment that the pupils will require?
- Are resources stored in a way which allows for quick retrieval?
- Are there clear policies, rules about behaviour in the classroom?
- Is there a set format for clearing up at the end of a lesson?

Source: Waterhouse (1990)

Monitoring and assessment

Effective teaching goes hand in hand with effective monitoring of the progress of a lesson and of pupils' learning. This is distinctive from evaluation which will be dealt with later. Monitoring refers to the way in which the teacher needs to assess routinely the progress of a lesson to ensure its success. In practice, many of the tasks carried out by the teacher during a lesson are part of the overall monitoring of learning. In considering those characteristics of monitoring a lesson which will lead to effective learning, the context of the lesson needs to be kept in mind. For example, the teaching approach adopted, the learning content selected and the range of pupils abilities will all have an effect on the type of monitoring of learning employed by the teacher.

Nevertheless, a number of characteristics of effective monitoring apply across a range of lesson types.

Effective monitoring

- The teacher is genuinely interested and concerned with each pupils progress
- The teacher's instructions are clear and the learners know what is expected of them
- The teacher uses good and varied questioning to monitor pupils' understanding and to raise the level of pupils' thinking
- The teacher monitors the progress of the lesson and adjusts it as necessary to ensure that it flows well and that pupils are engaged on task
- Pupil behaviour is monitored by the use of eye contact, questions and a change of lesson pace; potential misbehaviour is curtailed
- Lesson interruptions are kept at a minimum in order that the teacher can monitor learners more effectively

---

For inexperienced teachers monitoring can be both complex and demanding as it involves continuous decision-making about the next step. With experience, however, teachers become more adept in picking up the signals which indicate how a lesson is proceeding.

The skill of assessment is also important in maintaining effective monitoring in the classroom. Assessing pupils' progress during a lesson or throughout a piece of work can be achieved through a variety of means but is essential for effective learning to take place. The importance of tests, questions or essays, lies in the diagnostic information they provide for both learners and teachers. For the teachers, assessment provides a means of judging how learning is going and what exactly is being learned and by whom. For the learner, assessment is a crucial part of the overall feedback that learners need in order to judge the progress they are making. Research into effective departments has shown that the quality and frequency of the feedback given to pupils about their learning is an important determinant of effective learning because it is positively valued by pupils (Harris *et al*, 1994).

Whether done collectively or individually, feedback should be provided promptly. In giving feedback, the teacher needs first to establish what the learners' difficulties might be and how feedback can be best handled to meet individual learning needs. In this respect the feedback has to be diagnostic and focused on assisting learning rather than discouraging it. This means that feedback should be constructive and not destructive, it should be carefully handled so that the learner feels that there is a way forward. Finally, pupil feedback should be continuous and regular. Learners should expect it and value it as part of their target-setting cycle and their continuous learning.

Effective feedback should be:

- diagnostic
- regular
- soon after the task/work has been completed
- targeting areas for development
- constructive
- formative
- individually tailored

Reflection and evaluation

The twin processes of evaluation and reflection are essential for teachers to make them more effective. Evaluation is a process which necessarily involves the systematic collection of evidence and the making of informed judgements (English and Harris, 1992). Reflection, on the other hand, while less systematic is equally important if improvements in teaching are to be made. By reflecting on lessons and critically appraising them, important decisions about future teaching strategies can be made by the teacher. Research has shown that reflection is crucially important in improving teachers' professional practice (e.g. Schon, 1983, Calderhead, 1988).

Evaluating the effectiveness of a lesson involves a whole range of concerns. At one level the teacher will consider whether the intended learning outcomes have been effectively achieved. At another level, the teacher also needs to consider a host of very practical issues which largely focus on whether the lesson went as well as planned. Each teacher has intentions about their own teaching but unless they are monitored, it is difficult to know how well intention matches out-come.

Evaluating a lesson – Some questions teachers should ask

- How well did the lesson go generally? What were the highs and lows?
- What did the pupils learn in this lesson? How do I know what they learned?
- Were my intentions for this lesson met in full, in part, not at all? Why was this the case?
- Was any learner disadvantaged during the learning? How might this be avoided next time?
- What changes could be made to improve the lesson?
- Are there any immediate actions I need to take following the lesson?
- What did I learn from this about the way in which the lesson was structured, about the pupils, about the content, about the approach?
- How do I ensure that the learning which took place during the lesson is consolidated?
- Would I teach this lesson again?
- How might the lesson be taught differently? What might be the differences upon learners and learning?

Both reflection and evaluation are necessary for improvements in teaching and learning to be made. Without rigorous and systematic reflection there is a danger that complacency about learning will set in and ineffective lessons will ensue.

To summarise, the components of effective teaching are:

- Effective planning
- Meaningful learning
- A positive inter-personal climate
- Cognitive matching
- Translation
- Effective teaching time
- Quality of instruction
- High teacher and learner expectations
- Enhancing motivation
- Monitoring and assessment
- Reflection and evaluation

In linking effective schools and classrooms we should be concerned primarily with facilitating effective learning, which will be considered in the next section.

SECTION 6

Effective learning

INTRODUCTION

The previous section raised the question 'What is effective teaching?' and presented a model of teaching as an intentional, interactive process. This section poses two complementary questions: 'How do pupils learn?' and 'How can learning become more effective?' It is acknowledged that the literature concerned with both these questions is vast, and consequently this section attempts to highlight some of the relevant research findings and to describe several approaches to enhancing effective learning.

For much of this century, the question 'How do students learn?' has been answered in the behaviourist terms of stimulus and response. Learning was equated with conditioning, and it was believed that repeated practice and the use of rewards would help to elicit the appropriate response from the learner (Skinner, 1954; Hilgard, 1963). The last twenty years, however, have seen a dramatic shift in understanding the concept of effective learning. The stimulus–response tradition has been replaced with learning theories which view the learner as an active participant in the learning process. Theorists like Ausubel (1968) drew attention to the importance of the learner's pre-existing knowledge in determining what new information would be assimilated and how.

More recently, cognitive psychologists have drawn on clinical, experimental and survey-type research. Empirical work in this area has focused on individual skills, strategies, styles and approaches to learning (Marton, 1975; Marton, Hounsell and Entwistle, 1984; Marton and Saljo, 1976). This research work yielded two distinctive approaches to learning which were described as *deep level* and *surface level* processing. The deep approach was characterised as an active search for meaning. In contrast the surface approach tended to focus on specific facts, often memorised without understanding. In the UK this work has been complemented by that of Entwistle whose research findings showed that deep and surface approaches are two distinctive processes (Entwistle,1987; Entwistle, 1988). Comprehension learning (holism) was shown to be closely related to deep processing and operational learning (serialism) was shown to be a form of surface processing. It was argued that both strategies were necessary to achieve understanding.

Other research has emphasised the *context dependence* of effective learning. While there has been some confusion surrounding the idea of *teaching in a context*, it has been shown that embedding learning within a specified context enhances effective learning (Carraher *et al*, 1985; Stricht, 1989; Shanker, 1990). Similarly, analyses of the spectacular learning observed in young children has provided clues about effective learning (Bransford *et al*, 1985; Pea, 1989). This work has shown that effective learning takes place in context, that effective learning is often guided by parents, friends, or teachers and that the purpose of the learning is made explicit to the learner.

The research literature shows that effective learning always involves a modification of what the learner already knows or believes. What pupils are doing as they learn can be understood only in terms of the way in which their previous experience has prepared them to construe the new situation. Learning, therefore, can be guided and assisted successfully only in the light of this understanding. If what is taught does not engage the learner's current understanding in this way, it will be ignored, or, the learning will be ineffective (Claxton, 1984). The essence of effective learning lies in the ability of the teacher to edit, merge, split and relabel what learners already know and to move them forward from this position towards new learning.

The learners' minds are the only point of contact between what the school is offering and what they will take away with them in the way of comprehension, capability or quality. Consequently, effective teaching must take into account the implicit theories which learners already hold. These implicit theories can direct learners' attention and can channel their thoughts. These theories are often very stable and resistant to change. They can derive from three major sources; these are first-hand experience, informal social interaction and formal tuition, or teaching. It is important therefore, that these implicit theories are made explicit in order for learning to take place.

To learn effectively pupils need to be *effective gatherers, organizers and expressers* of knowledge. The main channels for gathering knowledge in school are: listening, reading, asking questions, and discussing. In acquiring knowledge successful learners adopt a stance of active interaction with the teacher and topic. They become engaged with the learning and actively seek ways of connecting together the various components of learning. One thing that distinguishes successful from unsuccessful learners is the ability to recognise and articulate what it is they do not know, or do not understand (Holt, 1984). The skill of being articulate about intellectual knowledge is an important strategy for amplifying that knowledge. It actually helps learners to learn as well as providing them with the ability to express what they know during exam time or during discussions and tests.

Guy Claxton (1990) in *Teaching to Learn* summarises the main conditions for effective learning to take place as follows:

> - All learners, pupils and teachers are in the business of making sense of the world around them. Effective learning means assisting pupils to make better sense of the world around them.
> - Knowledge is organised into mental packages or mini-theories that are developed to provide clear interpretation and smooth expertise in familiar domains of experience. Learning when to use what we know is as important a form of learning as increasing what we know.
> - Mini-theories are indexed not only according to the specific kinds of content to which they apply but also in terms of the complete social, emotional and physical context in which they have been developed.
> - Pupil learning varies not just in amount or in accuracy but in kind, depending on the knowledge that is available to them.
> - Much of teachers' influence on the development of pupil learning is achieved through their informal unguarded language and the implicit theories that they hold whether knowingly or not. If teachers are not themselves good learners they arrest both their own development and that of their pupils, via the implicit messages which they broadcast about what to value and what to fear.

Source: Claxton (1990)

APPROACHES TO EFFECTIVE LEARNING

As outlined earlier, learners learn in various ways and consequently a repertoire of teaching styles will be needed by the effective teacher. Some pupils are more comfortable with the written word, others find aural or visual material more accessible. Some pupils learn best through practical examples. Most people learn in all these ways to some extent. Teachers themselves are powerful role models who may exercise a profound influence for good or ill on pupils' achievements. The enthusiasm of a good teacher and the example of a good teacher are often the most important factors in motivating a pupil to learn and to want to learn. But even with an experienced and competent teacher, effective learning is not automatically achieved. Disaffected pupils can resist even the best teaching, just as effective learning can take place despite poor teaching.

Clearly the quality of learning can be improved for many more pupils by raising expectations about what they can achieve and by paying closer attention to their individual needs. Helping pupils to play a greater part in their own learning and making full use of resources both within and outside the school are important. Part of this process is equipping pupils with the *skills of learning how to learn* and offering them different learning contexts. Consequently, two approaches to developing the *skills of learning how to learn* will be outlined.

Thinking skills

Effective learning requires the development of thinking skills. Teachers need to create situations and tasks which encourage pupils to think hard in order to make progress. A recent approach to the teaching of science using activities designed to promote higher levels of thinking has been developed through the Cognitive Acceleration through Science Education Project (CASE). This approach has been trialled in a small number of schools around the country. It involves challenging children aged 11–13 to confront intellectual problems. Pupils are encouraged to think consciously about problem–solving so that they can generalise from their own experiences.

Both teachers and learners have to make conscious efforts to create bridges between newly learned principles and new contexts such as applying science learning to other subjects or to the world outside. To teach in this way teachers need to recognise the characteristics of higher–level thinking in order to help pupils develop reasoning patterns for themselves. The findings from this research show that the achievement of ordinary pupils in ordinary schools can be raised through a well-timed, well-targeted and well-delivered programme designed to develop the intellectual ability of pupils aged 11–13 years (Adey and Shayer, 1990). The research noted a profound and permanent effect on the children's ability to learn new material not only in science, the subject of the research, but also in mathematics and English. Consequently, there seems to be a strong case for the lessons derived from such work to be made more available to teachers. Clearly, improved thinking skills can make an important contribution to effective learning and thus to raising levels of achievement.

Flexible learning

The process of learning is as important as its content, since it often determines how much information and understanding is retained and the extent to which it can be applied in practice. The recognition that all learners are different supports a move towards flexible learning which acknowledges such individual differences. For example, individual differences include cognitive differences, i.e. differences in general intelligence, language skills, developmental readiness, problem-solving ability, critical thinking, and learning styles. There are personal differences, i.e. the pupils' general attitude to school and learning, emotional stability and motivation. Finally, there are social differences, i.e. differences because of different socio-economic backgrounds of family, friends and neighbourhoods.

One of the main arguments for flexible ways of organising learning is the range of individual differences and individual learning needs. Flexible learning uses a variety of learning techniques, e.g. small group tutorials, individual action plans and study guides. Pupils learn at their own pace with opportunities to go over material again or to move on as appropriate. By organising and using learning activities, environments and resources flexibly, teachers can then stimulate the capacity of learners to learn independently.

Flexible learning enables teachers to draw on a range of teaching styles to meet a wider range of individual needs. Concentrating on fixed pace, whole-class teaching can leave the learning requirements of many pupils unsatisfied. Relying on self-paced work can also result in low levels of achievement. Learning in groups can be more effective than either of these two approaches, if members of the group have the right mix of ideas and enthusiasm. Evidence from schools suggests that flexible learning is a good way of raising expectations and improving the quality of learning in the classroom. Yet it is important that pupils are emotionally and intellectually ready to take some responsibility for their own learning.

Confidence in studying independently provides the foundation for successful flexible learning and for learning throughout life. Supported self-study complements the use of flexible learning as well as helping institutions to respond to the increasing diversity of pupils' interests. In supported self-study the teacher helps pupils to plan the best use of study time, offering guidance, setting targets, organising pair and group work and assessing outcomes before planning the next stage. Better use of this non-contact time enables teachers to make more effective use of their time with pupils. This time can then be made more productive by using approaches which increase participation and motivation in students, e.g. presentations and group work.

The two central tenets of flexible learning are, first, an emphasis on learning by doing and, secondly, an emphasis on pupils' decision-making in the learning process. There is evidently a range of flexible learning techniques which can be used to support effective learning. Some of these techniques are summarised here:

Flexible learning techniques:

- Mini lectures prepared and given by individual pupils
- Debates – groups are formed to prepare and present opposing views
- Coaching – a learner is challenged to help another learner to achieve a high standard in some knowledge or skill
- Rehearsing – a learner or group practises a particular piece of learning until mastery is claimed
- Rounds – a way of making sure that everyone in a small group takes an active part
- Problem solving – all pupils identify a particular problem and write it down. This problem is then passed on to the next pupil. A short time is allowed for reflection and then each pupil in turn is asked to explain to the group the problem they have been given. They are also asked to suggest ways of solving it.
- Reviewing – a piece of work that has been done independently is reviewed by another pupil
- Team assessment – with a class organised in teams competing against one another in the learning process.

Both flexible learning techniques and the development of thinking skills emphasise three common elements of effective learning:

- The need to diagnose pupils' existing knowledge and understanding
- The need to develop different orientations and strategies of learning
- The need to develop the 'learning to learn' or metacognitive skills of students

This section has argued that effective learning is essentially an active process where new material is related to old and networks and connections are made between units of knowledge. To summarise:

- Effective learning is active rather than passive
- Effective learning is explicit rather than implicit
- Effective learning is complex rather than simple
- Effective learning is affected by individual differences amongst learners
- Effective learning is influenced by a variety of contexts

It therefore follows that effective learning is more likely to occur when:

- The teacher accurately diagnoses what the pupils already know
- The teacher consciously designs learning tasks that build from the pupils existing cognitive structures towards new knowledge or understanding to be acquired
- The teacher makes new knowledge and understanding meaningful to the pupils by linking it to personal experience or prior knowledge
- Pupils are given cues in advance to allow them to select and retrieve the existing knowledge they need to make sense of new inputs
- There is a match between pupils' preferred orientation to learning and the nature of the learning task
- Pupils are aware of their own learning strategies and learning preferences
- Pupils develop a repertoire of learning skills and strategies

The following section explores how effective learning is managed within the classroom and within schools.

The management of effective teaching and learning

INTRODUCTION

This section aims to bring together the research findings on whole school effectiveness (Part One) and the research findings on departmental and classroom effectiveness (Part Two). Recent research findings show that the effective management of schools is increasingly found to be influential for the learning and personal development of pupils (DFE, 1993). In essence, it suggests that school effectiveness can be linked to a particular set of management and teaching processes. Similarly, there is research evidence to confirm that effective schools do not just happen, but that they are effective because of the effective management structures which impact on the teaching and learning in the school (Fullan, 1991;1992).

Most of the early writing concerning effective teaching focused on the main aspects of teaching essential for success, namely the content and presentation of the lesson, classroom management, discipline and relationships with pupils. Such writing formed an early basis for the consideration of the expert knowledge about effective teaching (Kyriacou, 1986). This approach viewed teaching as a managerial activity and sought to identify the major tasks of teaching and the associated management activities required for effectiveness. Kounin's (1970) seminal work on classroom management drew attention to what appeared to be a number of managerial techniques employed by effective teachers in contrast to less effective teachers. Since then, two major strands of development have been pursued in school effectiveness studies.

- First, there has been an attempt to *identify* the management activities involved in effective teaching in terms of central teaching skills. There is an implicit assumption that managerial activities can be broken down into discrete component skills and that such skills can be fostered and developed within teacher education.
- Secondly, there has been an exploration of the *significance* of the various managerial activities for the teacher and pupils.

Successful school effectiveness projects have been seen to have both a wide and a narrow focus. Recently, it has been argued that the narrow focus of the *classroom* should be the main focus of research on school effectiveness, rather than the *whole school* (Brown *et al*, 1995). Small-scale developments in the classroom clearly have wider implications for the whole school and vice versa. If effective teaching and learning strategies are to be developed and implemented then the relationships between *micro level* of the classroom and the *macro level* of the school need to be explored.

If *change* and *learning* are similar processes, then *classroom* management and the management of *change* must have common features. A review of the relevant literature reveals that there are features, or principles, which are common to both fields. These features are shown below:

Effective classroom management and effective management of change involve:

- orchestration
- co-operation
- participation
- support
- a learning climate
- assessment

Each of these features will be discussed in turn.

Orchestration

As shown in Part One, leadership is an important factor in making schools more effective (*see* Southworth, 1990). The deployment, or *orchestration* of staff in the school is fundamental to effective management. Part One showed that the headteacher's leadership style is centrally important in the perceived and realised improvement of the school (Rutter *et al*, 1979; Mortimore *et al*, 1988; Southworth, 1990; Holly and Southworth, 1989). Learning outcomes are found to be more favourable when there is a combination of firm leadership with a decision making process in which all teachers feel that their views are represented. Effective headteachers, it has been shown, are adept at managing people, command trust and have high expectations of staff (Hopkins, 1986; Southworth, 1990; National Commission on Education, 1995).

Similarly in classrooms, responses from pupils are found to be more favourable when there is a combination of firm leadership from the teacher and where pupils feel that their views are represented. Effective teachers, like effective headteachers, are adept at managing pupils, command their trust and have high expectations of their pupils' potential achievement (Kyriacou, 1986). In addition, schools which are *improving* tend to be those in which the leadership style is characterised as consultative and where there is a sense of order and purpose. Similarly, recent research has shown that pupil achievement tends to be higher in classrooms where the teacher consults pupils about their learning and is receptive to pupils' ideas (Harris and Russ, 1994 a and b).

An effective teacher is generally characterised as someone for whom the well-being of pupils is the central focus. An effective headteacher also has been characterised in this way (Southworth, 1990). The effective headteacher is seen as someone who is able to motivate, inspire and challenge his or her staff but who takes ultimate responsibility in a crisis. Similarly, the effective teacher is someone who is able to motivate, inspire and challenge pupils but who takes ultimate responsibility for planning and orchestrating their learning.

Co-operation

In schools which are improving their performance, there exists a co-operative or collaborative team approach among the teaching staff (Rosenholtz, 1989; Fullan and Hargreaves, 1991; Lieberman, 1986; Stoll and Fink, 1992). In these schools, staff development is given a high profile and is viewed as an important means of introducing innovation and sustaining curriculum development. In the *improving* schools individual teachers are encouraged to be learners themselves, and staff are encouraged to collaborate in learning with and from, each other.

Teachers in 'effective' schools actively explore collaborative teaching approaches and tend to work co-operatively as a team (Harris and Russ, 1994; National Commission on Education, 1995). This team approach has been found to provide the environment in which learning can be articulated, tested, refined and examined against the needs of the organisation and within the context of the learning of others.

Co-operating and working with others is also central to the process of effective learning. In the classroom, effective pupil learning is viewed in broader terms than individual learning and group work is fundamentally important in fostering and developing alternative ways of learning. This co-operative or collaborative way of working with pupils can be characterised in the classroom in several ways. First, by attempts to involve all pupils in the learning process by providing a variety of tasks which deal with individual small group and large group situations. Secondly, by encouraging co-operative learning where pupils work together as part of a team, sharing experiences and being given different roles to develop their own self-esteem. Thirdly, by encouraging dialogue about learning with pupils and by engaging pupils in some form of action planning process which contributes to their learning. Finally, by teachers creating formative and motivational forms of assessment which reinforce pupil self-esteem and build confidence.

In effective schools, research has shown that individual teachers are encouraged to be learners themselves and staff are encouraged to collaborate by learning with and from, each other. This is clearly also the ethos of effective classrooms where working together is an important component of effective learning.

Active participation

Effective schools are those in which there are high levels of teacher commitment and sharing in the developmental learning process. Effective schools are 'learning schools' in the sense that staff either individually, or in small teams, work enterprisingly as learners. In these schools, staff work together as developers, evaluators and change agents on a variety of tasks which are orchestrated by senior management, rather than imposed upon them. Similarly, in effective classrooms, the teacher orchestrates learning by involving all pupils in the learning process through providing a variety of tasks which deal with the individual, small groups and large groups.

Effective schools are those in which there are high levels of teacher participation and where staff co-operate towards the shared aim of enhancing personal and professional development. Effective classrooms are those which encourage co-operative learning where pupils work together as part of a team sharing experiences, being given different roles and developing their own self-esteem. In effective classrooms pupils should have a sense of sharing in the learning process and be actively engaged in review and reflection upon learning. They need avenues for active participation in the learning process to become effective learners, just as teachers need to be participating actively in the work of the school if it is to be effective.

Support and reward

The previous section on effective learning highlighted the importance of support and reward in motivating learning and achievement. Research has shown that organising schools so that pupils are involved and are rewarded for their effort is very important (*see* case study B). Treating pupils with dignity and encouraging them to participate in the organisation of the school reassures them that they are valued. Giving ample opportunities for pupils to take responsibility and to participate in the running of the school leads to favourable learning outcomes. Similarly, teachers need to be rewarded and encouraged. They need to feel part of the school if they are to contribute to its effectiveness.

Therefore, for effective learning to take place, encouragement is essential along with a balance between support and challenge. As Joyce and Showers (1991) demonstrate the balance between support and challenge is also important in teacher development. Consequently, in effective schools staff need to feel motivated and supported. Similarly, in classrooms learners need to be given support and positive encouragement in order to learn effectively.

Learning climate

Research findings suggest that real school improvement can only be achieved through the re-conceptualisation of the school as a learning institution. This idea has already been promoted by several writers (Holly and Southworth, 1989; Jenkins, 1991; Southworth, 1994) and the learning institution is premised upon the notion that the school 'learns' its way forward, i.e. that the school is a 'learning system' (Schon, 1971). These research findings suggest that learning institutions need a learning climate which supports staff collaboration and in which the focus of that collaboration is centred on learning. This is also true of effective classrooms.

By comparison effective classrooms have a distinctive learning climate. In these classrooms there is a clear focus on teaching and learning, and this is the core purpose which drives all activity. Teachers are most successful and effective in the classroom when they are able to activate and manage the learning process through a variety of ways. For example, an emphasis on differentiation in teaching and learning styles provides pupils with easier access to the curriculum which clearly gives more opportunities for learning and achievement. In short, effective classrooms create a conducive learning climate for pupils and their work, and effective schools create a conducive learning climate for teachers and their work.

Planning and assessment

Effective schools establish a continual planning, implementation, monitoring and evaluation cycle which involves and supports staff (DFE, 1993). This provides guidance and direction for staff over time. Similarly, effective classrooms, establish a continual planning, implementation, observation and reflective learning cycle which supports pupils through the learning process. To have these recording and reviewing procedures firmly in place in schools is important in monitoring and identifying potential under-achievement.

In effective schools, mechanisms for monitoring pupil progress and self-evaluation are fully established and reinforced through both the academic and pastoral care systems. Information about the progress of individual pupils is also collected through a variety of means, on a regular basis and shared within and across departments/faculties.The monitoring and evaluation systems are fundamental to the quality of education being provided by the school and need to be embraced by both pupils and teachers.

Conclusion

The management of *change* and the management of *effective learning and teaching* are strikingly similar. The need for a system which contains both is central to any real school improvement. It is vital to ensure that the principles and practice that the staff are trying to achieve in their classrooms are mirrored in their own practice within the school as an organisation. It is no longer appropriate to talk in terms of particular individuals as change agents. All teachers are potential change agents.

Teachers need to harness their abilities and develop them as fully as possible. They spend a lot of time trying to produce a conducive climate for their pupils yet seem to apply none of the lessons learned from this exercise when dealing with other staff. Nevertheless the parallels are very clear. It is suggested, therefore, that these parallels should be more clearly established and used by schools to demonstrate that institutional changes are firmly grounded in good classroom practice. In this way new ideas or developments within institutions will not appear unrelated to teachers' experience but will connect with their own classroom practice. Conversely, institutions should actively promote and support teachers in introducing innovation and experimentation. This should be the basis for the direction and impetus of institutional change and development.

Effective schools and effective learners

To conclude Part Two, the key features of effective schools and effective learning are summarised as follows:

Effective schools	Effective learners
Understand how they develop as well as in what areas they are developing. They become instruments of their own development. They manage their own agenda for change and control their own development	Understand how they learn as well as what they learn. They become instruments of their own learning. They can manage and direct their own learning and make effective choices about how to learn
Operate within a framework of development which enables them to implement the statutory requirements through the appropriate teaching and learning approaches. They have the capacity to take ownership of imposed knowledge frameworks and to prevent their most damaging impact	Operate within a framework of learning which enables them to acquire skills, knowledge and understanding
Reflect on their development and systematically plan, do, review	Reflect on their own learning systematically and take stock of what they have learned and how they have learned it in order to plan for further learning
Are empowered—they have a belief in their own capacity to develop and to improve the school.	Are empowered—they have a belief in their capacity to shape their own learning effectively
Are task-focused and goal-orientated. They can marshal and manage resources to help them to achieve goals	Are task-focused and clear about their goals. They can handle resources for themselves as aids to their own learning
Can identify problems / areas for improvement, hypothesise about potential solutions, implement change and evaluate the effectiveness of the changes	Can raise questions / issues for themselves, hypothesise about potential solutions and test their hypotheses effectively in order to reach a conclusion
Can learn from previous experience and will allow that experience and the experiences of other schools to challenge the existing order. They regularly assess the way things are done in order to make judgements about their experiences and formulate ideas about what works or what might work more effectively	Can learn explicitly from previous experience, develop new conceptual understanding as a result and seek to test out that new understanding in order to develop further
Can evaluate their own performance effectively taking into account the judgement of others. They use their evaluations to shape their future actions and to help them to make choices about their future priorities	Can evaluate their own performance utilising the evaluations of others as part of the process. They use their evaluations to help them shape their future directions and to inform their choices about where to place their efforts in the future

PART THREE

Case studies

The purpose of Part Three is to offer case studies of school improvement in practice. The case studies have been selected to illustrate many of the ideas and principles covered in the previous sections. In this respect, the case studies are intended to be working examples, as they describe a wide range of school improvement initiatives. In the 'Halton' model (*see* Part One, p 43) it was suggested that school improvement took place at a number of different levels. Each of the case studies, therefore, describes school improvement initiatives operating at different levels and of varying scope and size.

While it is recognised that these case studies are context-specific, it is hoped that they can offer some ideas to assist other schools in the process of improvement:

- Case study A explores a wide-ranging set of improvement initiatives which were LEA led.
- Case study B considers the development of a reward and merit system designed to motivate pupils and to raise their self-esteem.
- Case study C focuses on strategies to improve pupils' performance at GCSE.

Dudley LEA

'RAISING STANDARDS IN INNER CITY SCHOOLS'

The challenge

The 'Raising Standards Project' began in the summer of 1991 as a result of an announcement of additional Government funding for inner city schools. Local Education Authorities were invited to bid for a portion of this funding, building their submissions around the central objective of *raising standards* and focusing particularly upon reading and home links. With the support of Local Education Authority (LEA) personnel and the commitment of several *inner city* schools, the Dudley submission was made.

Although Dudley had not qualified for inner city status, parts of the borough had many features associated with socio-economic deprivation. Consequently, the major goal of the submission was to improve the quality of educational provision for children in the most deprived area of the borough. It was anticipated that this goal would be achieved through the co-ordinated effort of schools and the local community. The full support of the LEA was also guaranteed.

The response to the challenge

The Dudley bid was successful and the money was awarded in 1992. This enabled a Project Director to be appointed and four schools (an 'inner city' secondary school and its feeder primary schools) to be involved in the project. The two-fold first task facing the Director was to identify the aims and objectives of the project, and to decide how these aims might be translated into practice. The three project aims were identified as follows:

1 Raising reading standards.
2 Developing learning strategies.
3 Increasing parental involvement and support.

It was acknowledged that the translation of these aims into practice would vary from school to school. In view of this, action plans were devised to suit each school's unique context with regard to facilities, staffing and stages of development. The appointment of project staff was subsequently made to respond to schools' needs and expectations. In the primary schools such appointments included Community Organisers and Project Assistants with a specific project brief. In the secondary school, a Study Tutor, a Home Liaison Support Teacher and a part-time library assistant were appointed to assist the project development.

There were a wide variety of initiatives which emerged in direct response to the project's three main aims. Details of these initiatives appear in Appendix 1, and have been broadly grouped under the three aims. As it is impossible to consider all of these initiatives , this case study will focus only on the first project's aim, i.e. Raising Reading Standards.

Aim one— raising reading standards

The aim was translated by the schools in the project into three key objectives.

1 To develop a positive pupil attitude towards reading.
2 To provide a structure within which pupils' reading skills could be monitored and developed.
3 To provide extra support for pupils experiencing difficulty with reading.

In order to meet the first objective of promoting a positive attitude towards reading, a number of school developments took place. These were carried-out cross-phase and included:

- setting up book boxes in the school
- working to make the libraries more attractive places
- spending money on new and exciting books

All the activities were designed to raise the status of reading in the schools and to extend parental involvement in their children's reading processes.

Other developments aimed at generating more pupil interest in reading included the setting up of a Reporter's Club and a Cookery Club. Both clubs focused on the books produced in that particular genre and were intended to promote pupils' interest in reading and writing. Similarly, the instigation of an 'Early Birds Club', which began at 8.30am, meant that pupils were able to come into school, sit in comfortable chairs and read quietly. In addition, pupils were also encouraged to keep a reading diary for the duration of the project.

Other initiatives which evolved from the project included:

- paired reading, where older children were paired with younger children
- the development and use of reading games designed to support curriculum subjects
- extra research in phonics, to support a whole-book policy, was also part of the professional development programme for teachers in the schools
- funding was made available to give members of staff time to discuss and write whole-school reading policies. This ensured that reading practice and policy affected the whole school curriculum

Activities which involved parents in raising children's awareness of reading were also centrally important to the project. Parents were invited to school to listen to their children reading. To ensure maximum coverage the schools varied the time parents could come to the school to hear their children read. In addition, liaison between the bilingual support worker and Asian parents was encouraged and given a high priority. To date, a large number of parents continue to support this target group of children in their reading.

Aims Two and Three

The second objective, namely to provide a structured framework for reading development, and the third objective, to provide support for reading development were not viewed as mutually exclusive. Instead a number of activities were set up to address both these objectives simultaneously.

The first activity involved the Wellington Square Scheme. This was a structured reading scheme aimed to support poor readers which was introduced into the secondary school. The intention was to provide the basis for working with poorer readers in small groups. In this scheme pupils were withdrawn from lessons to work in small groups using the Wellington Square material. The scheme provided books, worksheets and audio cassettes and used a range of strategies to encourage pupils to read independently. The scheme was well supported by school staff, some giving their free time to work with groups on the material. The scheme was subsequently introduced to Year 6 pupils in the primary schools, thus ensuring cross-phase continuity.

The second activity involved the New Zealand Reading Recovery programme. This was another programme designed to develop the reading skills of weak readers within an organised framework. In this programme children were trained to become independent readers through decoding the print on the page by using things like the reading context, or the letter sound. From the initial stages children were encouraged to think for themselves and to use all the means at their disposal to work out words or phrases. In this respect reading was seen as a problem-solving exercise.

To be recruited to the scheme children's chronological ages had to be between 5 years 9 months and 6 years 3 months. They were then seen on a one-to-one basis every day for a period of thirty minutes. During each session a child would read four or five books, would write, would work with magnetic letters and develop his or her spelling patterns. The programme aimed to take the four children with the weakest reading skills within the designated age ranges and within twenty weeks to bring them to a level of reading deemed to be equal to that of the class average. There was evidence that by the end of the programme this had been achieved.

Evidence of success

In October 1993, HMI gave a positive appraisal of the Dudley Project and commented favourably on the number and variety of initiatives in place. In relation to the project's first aim, the schools found evidence of major improvement in children's reading. For example, some of the Year 7 pupils who had systematically worked with the Wellington Square Scheme had raised their reading age by two to three years. These reading ages had been measured by the Suffolk Reading Test prior to, and following, the pupils' involvement in the Wellington Square Scheme.

The success of the Reading Recovery work is still to be evaluated, though several indications of success are in evidence. For example, from the initial training of one teacher in the use of the scheme at the very start of the project, thirty-three teachers were subsequently trained as Reading Recovery teachers. Similarly, of the six children who worked on the scheme each term, there was a general progression from Level 1 to Level 15. Other evidence of two reading groups who were monitored between 1992 and 1993 showed a 38 per cent success rate and 61.5 per cent success rate. There was also evidence of writing improvement amongst these pupils.

Similarly, there was an indication of the project's success in involving parents in supporting young readers by their attendance at reading sessions in the school. For example, at one primary school, 40 per cent of the target group continued to support their children over the whole year period. Consequently, increased parental involvement in supporting children's reading was an important outcome of the project. A Curriculum Newsletter issued in the primary schools became a termly, not annual letter, because it was identified by parents as 'valuable'.

Advice to other schools

1 Where reading policies do not exist, time has to be allocated for their development.
2 INSET training and whole school planning are essential pre-requisites for developing a whole school reading policy.
3 Materials used in subject curriculum areas need to be reviewed with a focus on readability.
4 Schools need to involve parents in whatever ways they can, to provide children with reading support in their home.
5 Involving parents of the Year 7 group is an essential step. If they are involved as equal partners at an early stage then there will be greater possibility of their continued involvement in the school.
6 Schools must be prepared to make changes to their ways of working with parents. They need to be more flexible to ensure that they respond to the particular needs and concerns of parents within this deprived community.
7 Initiatives which constantly promote reading, which can be used to raise general awareness, are essential. These initiatives need to have narrow foci and run for short periods so that enthusiasm and staff energy will be maintained.
8 The challenge of raising reading standards may well be multi-faceted, with lots of small initiatives going on within classrooms, departments, across schools, for short periods, in every possible way.
9 Use external agencies to promote and fund school initiatives.
10 It is important that specified members of staff take responsibility and are accountable for each improvement initiative.

Reflection and analysis

In analysing this case study there are some important elements of school improvement which have been highlighted earlier in this book:

1 The climate for change Funding helped to create a climate within which improvement happened. Change needed to be actively embraced by the participants in it and managed by external agents employed by the project.

2 Management of change	The Project Director and Team recognised from the outset that school colleagues needed to 'own' the initiatives. They also accepted that at some point school colleagues expected the team to lead and push forward the initiatives. This project was able to integrate team members into schools through attendance at staff meetings, curriculum planning meetings and through their involvement in staff development sessions. The process of change had two foci, firstly project team members working with school colleagues to facilitate change, secondly project members working independently to initiate and press for agreed changes to be carried out.
3 The scope of change	The Project's aims were translated into specific initiatives and suitable staff were appointed to match the needs of those initiatives. Hence, whilst the scope of the change was varied and extensive the initiatives within this broad scope were manageable and small-scale.
4 Monitoring and evaluating change	The process of monitoring and evaluation was used formatively to affect change during the project and to provide feedback on progress.
5 Pupil learning	Strategies used to support weak readers maximised effective learning time by using structured programmes. Additionally these programmes aimed to encourage learners to become independent learners.
6 Parental involvement	Continuous information flow to parents through newsletters was a feature of this project and was practised by all the schools. The project identified the need to engage parents as equal partners in their children's learning and recognised the need to be sensitive and responsive to cultural differences.

APPENDICES TO CASE STUDY A

Appendix 1

The project plan

Raising Standards Project
1992–1995

The Dudley Project involves 1 secondary and 3 primary schools committed to raising standards of teaching and learning:

Project aims: to raise pupils' achievement in the core subjects through an emphasis on:

- improving reading skills
- developing learning strategies
- increasing parental involvement and support

LDE/SC 2.2.93

Raising Standards Project
1992–1995

Project objectives:

- to develop positive attitudes towards reading
- to provide a structure within which pupils' reading skills can be monitored and developed
- to provide extra support for pupils experiencing difficulty with reading
- to provide environments and resources which facilitate pupils' study out of school hours as well as in the classroom
- to make Information Technology an integral part of children's learning
- to promote active learning
- to develop a community curriculum
- to improve parents' awareness of their role in education
- to facilitate parental support

Raising Standards Project
1992–1995

Improving reading skills

- to develop positive attitudes towards reading
- to provide a structure within which pupils' reading skills can be monitored and developed
- to provide extra support for pupils experiencing difficulty with reading

shared reading

new books

book club

classroom support

Reading Recovery

Wellington Square

Busy Bee Club
Climbers Club

Phonics

5 o'clock Club
Super Readers

INSET

Reading diaries

Appendix 1 (contd.)

Raising Standards Project
1992–1995

Developing learning strategies

- To provide environments and resources which facilitate pupils' study out of school hours as well as in the classroom
- To make Information Technology an integral part of children's learning
- To promote active learning

Study Centre

Community rooms

Library

I.T. Equipment

I.T. INSET

Classroom support

Extended day

GRASP

Study sessions

Reading games and activities

Raising Standards Project
1992–1995

Increasing parental involvement and support

- To develop a community curriculum
- To improve parents' awareness of their role in education
- To promote active learning

RSP Meetings

Community Rooms

Parent helpers

IMPACT

Parents at after-school clubs

Home visits

Pre-nursery group

Workshops

Shared reading

Appendix 2

Project aims and initiatives

AIM ONE: RAISING READING STANDARDS
Initiatives included:

(a) shared reading sessions with parents
(b) extra teaching for poorer readers
(c) reading recovery programme

AIM TWO: LEARNING STRATEGIES
Initiatives included:

(a) lunchtime and after school clubs as part of an extended day
(b) study sessions
(c) the development of a study centre in a re-furbished community room or within a library area
(d) support in classrooms for weak pupils
(e) support in classrooms for able children
(f) Information Technology within classrooms and the school

For staff development, four major developmental programmes were proposed:

(a) differentiation
(b) developing a community curriculum
(c) teaching reading
(d) understanding and using IT

Additionally, across the four participating schools time and money was allocated to:

(a) school reviews
(b) the development of reading policy
(c) support was given to individuals which enabled them to attend relevant courses and conferences

AIM THREE: INCREASING PARENTAL INVOLVEMENT AND SUPPORT
Initiatives included:

(a) IMPACT (Involvement in Maths for Parents and Children and Teachers, Mother and Toddler Group)
(b) Parenting skills work

Appendix 2 (contd.)

(c) Mother and Toddler Group

(d) Reading workshops for parents

(e) Parent child teacher contracts

(f) Developing adult learning in IT

(g) Supporting adult literacy classes

(h) Encouraging links with the Technical College

(i) Developing a community room which can be used by adult members of the community

(j) A bi-lingual project worker was able to involve parents of minority ethnic groups

(k) There has been a substantial amount of refurbishment to community facilities and study areas

(l) Books, toy library equipment, expendable materials and IT equipment were acquired and are in daily use in lessons, in after school clubs and Saturday clubs.

Appendix 3

This appendix has included a sample of the range of communications sent to parents and given to the pupils.

Involving parents and pupils in the range of activities the project offered

---

Curriculum Newsletter

Spring Term 1994

RSP 1994

Some dates for your diary ...

- 1st February ~
  Mother and Daughter Group
  Years 5 & 6 – 2.45 p.m.

- 11th February ~
  School closes for half term holiday

- 22nd February ~
  School re-opens at 9.00 a.m.

- 25th March ~
  School Disco

- 30th March ~
  Parents' Evening 7–9 p.m.

- 31st March ~
  End of term
  School closes at 3.30 p.m.

How you can help

- Read with your child several times each week.

- Talk with them about their school topics.

- Teach them new words related to their topic.

- Visit the library and help them choose books about their topic. Make sure they're not too difficult!

- Don't be afraid to try out activities e.g. growing seeds, model making.

- Practising times tables 2 × 2, 3 × 3...

- Have you or your family any items that can be used in topic work e.g. photographs, old fashioned objects?

- Have you got special skills or knowledge that you could share with any of the age groups in school?

If you need more information please talk to your child's class teacher

Appendix 3 (contd.)

NURSERY

Colours Learning about a different colour each week through stories, songs, rhymes etc. Wednesday is dressing up day for the theme colour.

EARLY PHASE

Reception

- colour
- snow
- wind
- rain
- clothes

A series of short topics which children will learn about through a variety of activities

Year 1

- Toys old and new, sorting and grouping, exploring how toys move.
- Measures comparing lengths using handspans etc. Weighing objects with stones, bottle tops etc.

Year 2

- Beginnings animal life, plants, dinosaurs.
- Measures weight, length, time, comparing, ordering and measuring.

MIDDLE PHASE
Years 3 & 4

Invaders and Settlers

Romans, Vikings and Saxons. Finding out about the reasons for invasion.
Comparing family life.
In depth study of one of the invaders.

Local Study

Finding out about settlement, land use, buildings etc., in the local area.

Forces

Finding out about push and pull in everyday life.

Investigating rolling things, friction, floating and sinking and structures.

UPPER PHASE
Years 5 & 6

Families, childhood and home life.

Comparing the everyday life of the Ancient Greeks, the Tudors and Stuarts and families in the 1950's

- Mapwork skills – reading, using and making maps.

- Families and communities.
  In depth study of life in
  Ladak – Tibet,
  Chemba Kohli – India and
  Kenya – Africa.

- Ourselves and Health Education.

  Finding out about healthy living and how we grow and develop.

- Electricity

  Investigating circuits and switches. Making simple electrical devices.

Appendix 3 (contd.)

Developing learning strategies at primary level

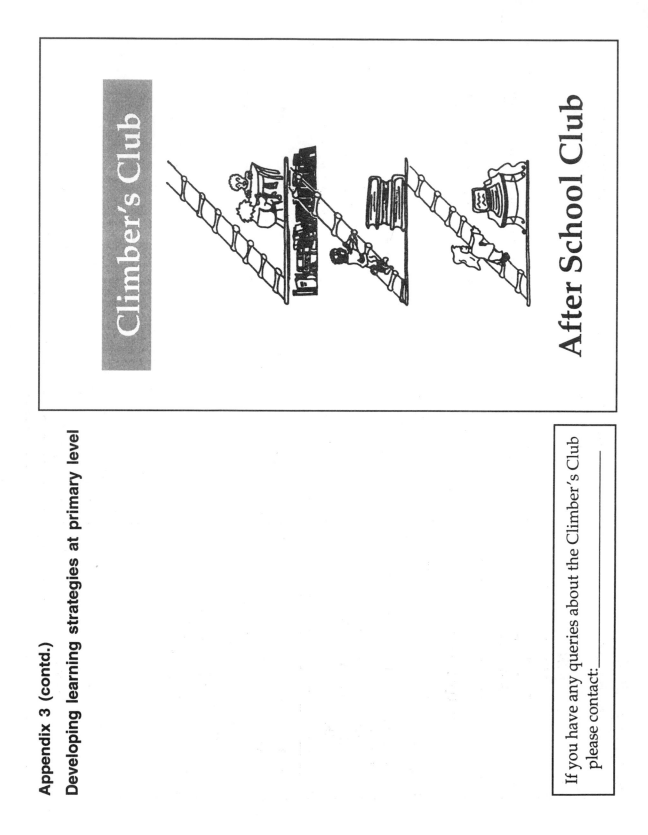

Climber's Club

After School Club

If you have any queries about the Climber's Club please contact:_____

Appendix 3 (contd.)

Where is the Club ?

In the Library

What times does it start and finish ?

It starts at 3.30 pm and ends at 4.30 pm.

12 3
9 6
Start

12 3
4
9 5
6
End

What can I do in the Climber's Club ?

Lots of things:-

read
play games
work on the computer
listen to a story
finish off some work
spelling
handwriting
topic work

There will always be a teacher there to help you.

Appendix 3 (contd.)

Improving reading and involving parents in this process

"Reading Together"

We want the children at our school to be good readers.
We will do our best. Will you help too?

Our promise

1. *To provide suitable books for your child to read.*
2. *To teach the basic skills necessary for successful reading.*
3. *To hear you child read regularly.*
4. *To keep you informed of your child's progress.*

Your promise

1. *To find 5 minutes each day to share my child's book.*
2. *To help my child to take care of the reading book.*
3. *To remind my child to bring the pack to school each day.*
4. *To encourage and support my child by praising every effort he or she makes.*

School signature ....

Home signature .... *Date* ....

Appendix 3 (contd.)

Developing learning strategies at secondary level

Study Sessions

What can I do in these study session?

- homework or finishing off classwork
- reading
- spelling, handwriting
- GCSE coursework
- finding information – from books or from the computer
- work on the computers

There will always be at least one teacher present to help you with your work if you need it.

Where are the study sessions held?

- In the Library

    and

- In room J11

What time are the study sessions?

- at lunchtime – between 12.25 and 1.20 pm Everyday
- after school – between 3.30 and 5.00 pm. Monday – Thursday

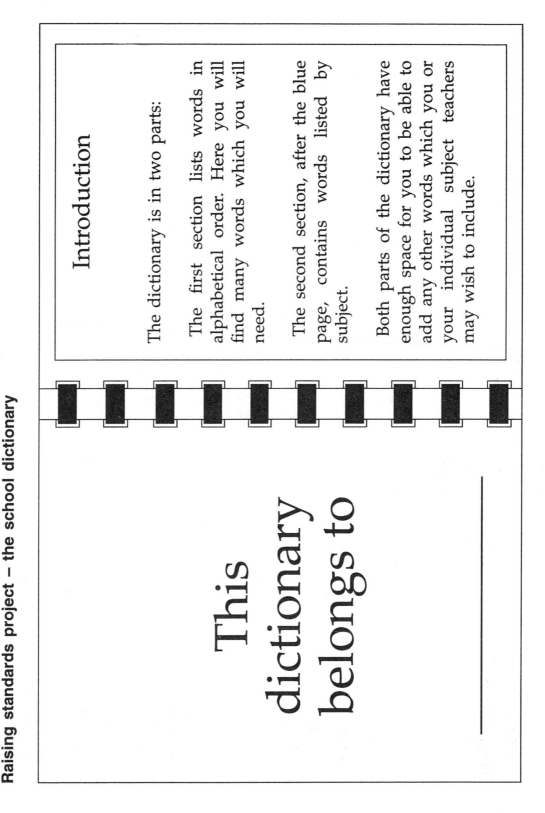

Introduction

The dictionary is in two parts:

The first section lists words in alphabetical order. Here you will find many words which you will need.

The second section, after the blue page, contains words listed by subject.

Both parts of the dictionary have enough space for you to be able to add any other words which you or your individual subject teachers may wish to include.

This dictionary belongs to

Dd

dance	disk
danger	dissolve
dark	distillation
data	Divali
database	divide
date	division
daughter	do
day	document
decimal	does
defence	doesn't
definitely	dog
delivery	doing
deputy	doll
describe	Domesday Book
description	done
development	don't
diagonal	door
diary	down
did	draw
didn't	drawing
difference	drill
different	drink
dig	drive
dimensions	drone
diminuendo	Dudley
dinner	
disappear	
disc	
disco	

Pp

painting	plane	project
paper	plastic	prototype
parallel	play	public relation
parallelogram	please	pull
parliament	plenty	pulse
part	plural	push
party	poem	put
pastel	poet	
pen	point	
pencil	police	
pentatonic	policeman	
people	policewoman	
percussion	political	
perimeter	pollen	
permanent	pollination	
perpendicular	pollution	
personal	poor	
phone	prayer	
photo	predicting	
phrase	present	
physical	pretty	
piano	printer	
pictorial	printing	
picture	priory	
pig	Priory Road	
pipette	private	
pitch	processing	
place	processor	
plain	product	

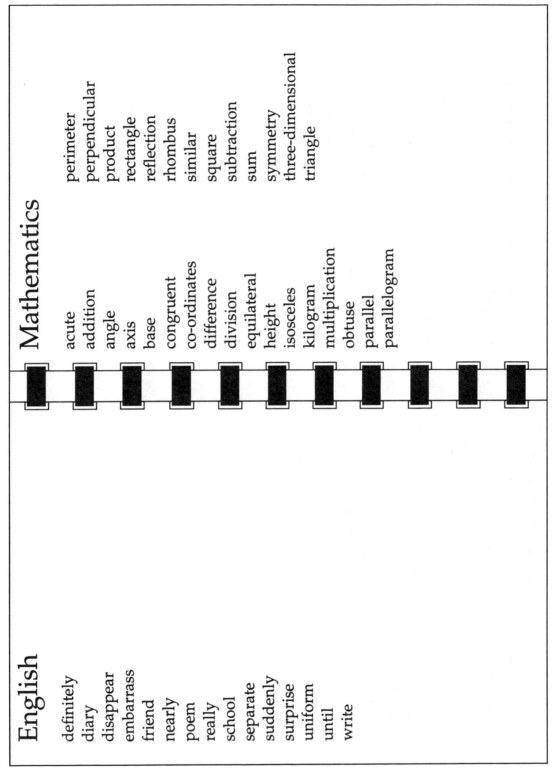

English

definitely
diary
disappear
embarrass
friend
nearly
poem
really
school
separate
suddenly
surprise
uniform
until
write

Mathematics

acute
addition
angle
axis
base
congruent
co-ordinates
difference
division
equilateral
height
isosceles
kilogram
multiplication
obtuse
parallel
parallelogram

perimeter
perpendicular
product
rectangle
reflection
rhombus
similar
square
subtraction
sum
symmetry
three-dimensional
triangle

Appendix 4 (contd.)

Samples from subject pages (continued)

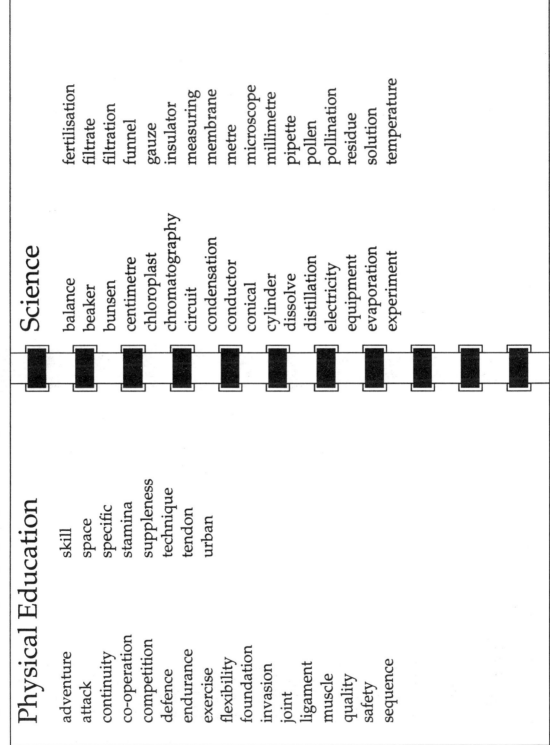

Physical Education

adventure
attack
continuity
co-operation
competition
defence
endurance
exercise
flexibility
foundation
invasion
joint
ligament
muscle
quality
safety
sequence

skill
space
specific
stamina
suppleness
technique
tendon
urban

Science

balance
beaker
bunsen
centimetre
chloroplast
chromatography
circuit
condensation
conductor
conical
cylinder
dissolve
distillation
electricity
equipment
evaporation
experiment

fertilisation
filtrate
filtration
funnel
gauze
insulator
measuring
membrane
metre
microscope
millimetre
pipette
pollen
pollination
residue
solution
temperature

Appendix 5

Projection evaluation, June 1994: evidence of success

(Extract from the final report on the Dudley Project, June 1994, by the Research Development and Evaluation Unit)

5.0   Findings

5.1   The oral report given by the HMI's at the end of their visit in October 1993 was summarised by Linda Evans and circulated to all interested parties. There were a number of very positive statements about the Project, of which the principal were:

i)   The extra funding had obviously given a boost to the four schools, where there was evidence of rapid change and improvement.

ii)   Project staff, commended for their commitment and enthusiasm, were well timetabled, with good acountability.

iii)   In-service training for Project staff was being put to effective use.

iv)   Lunchtime and after-school clubs, at which attendance was high, were well structured and complementary to the school curriculum.

v)   Good links were developing with parents.

iv)   Management of the Project was efficient with effective liaison and support.

5.2   The four Heads all expressed great satisfaction with the Project, lamenting only the abrupt ending of its funding. An experienced Head still considered it a 'learning experience' and another was pleased with its knock-on effects among the staff. Not merely the funding, but the selection, ordering and the general administration of resources – books in particular – were widely appreciated. Though there had been a strong focus on less able pupils, the opportunities for work with able pupils had also given an impetus to the Project that was greatly valued.

5.3   Interviews

During January and February 1994 a series of interviews were held with some of the teaching staff of the Project schools, the pupils and the parents of pupils who participated in the Project's activities. Absences through illness slightly limited the numbers. Some parents were interviewed in their homes.

	Staff	Parents	Pupils
School A	2	2	2
School B	4	2	2
School C	2	3	4
School D	6	4	4

The comments of parents were particularly forthright and interesting. Pupils tended to express briefly their enjoyment of the activities. Teachers confirmed the work of the activities but sometimes saw them from a new perspective. The perceptions of the Project are summarised below under the four schools.

Appendix 5 (contd.)

5.3.1 School A

The mother of a year 3 boy commented on the after-school Climbers Club enthusiastically: 'He loves Climbers. He loved doing plays and making pots with clay. It teaches them to sit still. He used to get up after two minutes at home.' The boy also helps in the stationery shop, recently established with much planning and help from the children. 'He enjoys it. Helps with money and maths in giving change. Helped with talking to people.'

A mother with three daughters at the school echoed this maturing influence of the clubs: Of the year 2 daughter in the Climbers 'Makes her more mature and independent' and of the year 3 daughter in the Chess Club and Busy Bee Club 'I think it's brought her out of herself.'

A teacher of year 5/6 considered that many children, formerly underachieving, had made great progress since the start of the Project and believed that 'clubs stimulate children for normal classroom work.' Saturday Club in particular 'has brought benefit to children who would have done little themselves at home.'

A teacher of years 4/5 stressed the value of 1–1 reading support, spoke highly of Early Risers – 'gives the extra it's hard to offer in a class of 30' – and saw the clubs giving benefit to indigenous children in teaching them to play games and in particular in giving the experience of visits and trips to Asian girls who in some cases might expect only to do housework.

5.3.2 School B

The mother of two boys expressed satisfaction at the Project. The year 4 boy found that in the Community Room 'lunchtime was more relaxing' and the year 6 boy in the 5 o'clock club enjoyed 'an atmosphere that is not strictly school.' The mother of a year 4 girl who had missed 3 months schooling in an earlier year said that she 'never seemed to catch up until she joined the Super Readers Club. She's really come on wonderfully.'

The year 1 teacher who assists with drama, a joint venture between RSP staff and the school's Creative Arts Team, saw it as an opportunity to meet older children and to take part in a whole-school activity. Two other teachers remarked on the benefit of the Super Readers and Drama Clubs: children enjoyed having someone other than a parent or class teacher listening to them reading.

The Panda Club, established with RSP funds enabled children to gain the fullest benefit from the Nursery Group by coming to the school campus and getting to know staff. Nursery staff in turn could get to know mothers in the relaxed surroundings of the Community room.

Appendix 5 (contd.)

5.3.3   School C

The mother of three boys in years 3, 5 and 6, all attending the Books and Boards Club, commented enthusiastically 'They really look forward to it. It learns them to play with one another.' Another mother of a year 5 boy whose reading had improved had praise for the library: 'All children like the library, all eager to get a book. They seem to know what they want.' Another mother who attends and helps, said her son enjoyed the lunchtime Music and Movement.

Two year 2 pupils thought lunchtime games 'lots of fun' and a year 6 boy enjoyed Chess and Drama – 'It's fun because you get to do a lot of different things like an argument or a fight.' A year 6 girl enjoyed doing homework based on 'Danny, the Champion of the World'.

Both teachers interviewed felt that the children's speaking and listening skills had improved from attending a club like Books and Boards. The reception teacher enthused over the Reading Together scheme where parents read regularly with the children. The clubs were seen as an outlet for energy without disrupting others and an opportunity for a teacher to get to know children in the year before they came into her class.

5.3.4   School D

The parents interviewed, all with children in year 7, expressed great satisfaction with the school in general and with their children's progress in particular. The mother and father of a girl commented: 'Her reads well now. Her spends her money all on books' and 'She wants to go to school – she'd go Saturdays and Sundays if she could.' Both these parents and another mother expressed pride in certificates gained and a letter from the school indicating the daughter's high marks in tests" 'Her reading is learning her how to spell better.'

The mother of a boy had seen a great improvement in reading and attitude: 'He comes home and does his homework – no problem. Willing to go into public library and bring books home to read. Five months ago, no chance.'

Opinions on the school in general were equally positive: 'They are really building his confidence up. We can see such a difference in him.' The mother of a girl summarised the two obvious benefits of the homework club, a quiet environment and the chance to have uncertainties resolved: 'Homework club is really a good idea where she can concentrate. At home it's difficult to stop the others plaguing her' and 'There's always someone there to explain.'

These advantages of the homework club were echoed by all four of the pupils interviewed. Two remarks were 'I can do my homework quicker here', 'It's quieter than at home.'

Appendix 5 (contd.)

All six teachers interviewed thought highly of the Project and again the homework club was mentioned: 'I can say to a pupil; "Go along there. I'll meet you", and I can go over something in a pleasant, relaxed working environment with resources.' Other teachers praised the quality of the books purchased under the Project and the established arrangements for RSP staff to make home visits. The other activities – the Science Club, the School Musical, the poetry anthology by year 7 pupils for example – were all appreciated by staff.

Four Dwellings School

REWARD AND MERIT SYSTEM

The school context

Four Dwellings Comprehensive School is an 11–18 school within Birmingham, which borders on Sandwell LEA. Its geographical position has meant that parents have the choice to send their children to schools within Sandwell LEA. The choice of schools in the neighbouring LEA includes two girls' schools and one boys' school. This has meant that an increasing number of parents have sent their children to Sandwell. Consequently, Four Dwellings School has experienced falling roles.

Viewed as a neighbourhood school, Four Dwellings School has been supported by a loyal cohort of parents, mostly those who attended the school themselves. The community served by the school is largely manual working class, with some semi-skilled and skilled workers. The school has between 45–60 per cent of pupils who are entitled to free school meals, so generally it is acknowledged that the school is located within a relatively poor socio-economic context. The Deputy Head described the school as one which offered a caring environment for its pupils but a school in which pupils' achievement was a cause for concern amongst staff.

The challenge

With the advent of parental choice, local management of schools (LMS) and the publication of school examination league tables, it was evident that the school needed to promote and market itself to avoid a further fall in rolls. Associated with this was a general staff desire to raise levels of achievement within the school. At the same time a new Deputy was appointed with the working brief to market the school and develop a system through which positive pupil achievement could be recognised. One of the challenges which the school set itself, therefore, was *to develop a system which recognised and rewarded pupil achievement in order to improve the school and to increase its recruitment.*

Response to the challenge

A crucially important starting point in meeting the challenge was the Deputy Head's recognition of the need to begin at pupil level. He subsequently gathered together a volunteer group of between 12–14 children, of different ages and reputations within the school, to talk with him about *how they thought the level of achievement could be raised within the school.* Apart from the Deputy Head no other teachers were involved in these initial discussions. The pupils and Deputy brainstormed their ideas and eventually narrowed them down to focus upon one particular aspect which was *how more recognition could be given to children who did their homework?* Other issues were raised, but the group decided that homework was the priority. It became evident that pupils were regularly doing homework but felt that they needed some certification, or system of feedback from teachers to acknowledge that they were submitting good-quality work. They felt that they needed a system which recognised both the level of effort and the achievement contained in the homework submitted.

At this stage the Deputy talked with the pupils about getting some sponsorship for the project and with agreement from them he approached Cadbury's who had a good reputation for supporting community initiatives. A Director of Cadbury's became convinced about the value of the initiative and agreed to support the development. It was at this stage that all staff became involved and it was jointly decided that the initiative should commence in Year 7.

The process: Homework Merit and Award Scheme

The resulting Homework Merit and Award Scheme comprised the following:

1 At seven weekly intervals staff in the nine subject areas commented on pupils efforts in relation to homework.
2 This was recorded by the Deputy on a spreadsheet.
3 Commendations were supported by letters of congratulations to parents.
4 All commendations contributed to an end-of-term and end-of-year award at bronze level (7 commendations) , silver level (8 commendations) and gold level (9 commendations).
5 A final stage—the celebration of achievement evening during which
    a) certificates of outstanding performance;
    b) the Cadbury trophy;
    c) the Cadbury shield
    were presented.

(*See* Appendices for further details of the scheme)

In September 1990 the Cadbury Award Scheme began and the improvement process unfolded. Within that first seven weeks all children in Year 7 had received a letter home which complimented them on their homework. The letter also encouraged them to improve on their performance next time around. This scheme quickly gathered momentum and pupils in Year 7 were soon saying *We should do this for all years*.

Consequently, the scheme was extended into homework across all years in the school. By the following September the pupils felt that the scheme should be extended into the area of classwork. The pupils felt that there might be something different needed for Years 10 and 11, but the key criterion remained that it had to be a system that was fair, that rewarded the pupils for achievement measured against their own particular standards.

As the scheme was extended into classwork as well as homework, it became apparent which departments were awarding commendations. So, additionally, the Deputy was able to gather information which would give insights into the reward and praise systems of individual subject departments within the school. This information was used at a later stage in the other developments.

As part of the celebration of this success certificates were produced and presented to the children at year assemblies. When a pupil achieved a maximum of 21 commendations he/she was awarded the Cadbury Trophy Level One for Achievement. If this award was achieved three times in a school year the pupil kept the trophy. To date, despite the number of trophies the children are receiving, Cadbury's remain committed to the reward scheme.

For pupils in Years 10 and 11 a different reward scheme was developed, deliberately aimed at motivating pupils to improve their GCSE performance. The scheme was a seven-point scale, the top of the scale being Point 1, which was identified as 'keeping well on top of classwork and homework expectations' while Point 7 was 'very serious concern exists about the lack of classwork and homework contributions'. Letters to parents made them aware of the scheme and kept them informed of their child's efforts. Within this scheme pupils still received gold, silver and bronze awards.

Developments from the Cadbury Scheme

The enthusiasm for the scheme on the part of both pupils and staff led to its extension into other areas. The scheme currently covers five areas; Homework, Classwork, Attendance, Punctuality and Behaviour. It was felt that the better the children performed in all these areas the more successful would both teaching and learning become.

The latest development of the Cadbury Scheme was a focus on pupil conduct, that is, behaviour, which commenced in 1993. Once again pupils were asked for their input by completing diaries with the question in mind 'What helps you to learn and what prevents you from learning?' In addition, staff were interviewed anonymously about what they felt prevented learning. The analysis of these interviews resulted in a Behaviour Code, which went into all classrooms. The Behaviour Code was then endorsed by a Cadbury's Conduct Award.

A valuable feature of the award scheme was the evidence that was collected. The spreadsheet evidence which recorded all the commendations across the five areas of the Award Scheme was available to any pupil, teacher, any parent or member of the Senior Management Team. This spreadsheet enabled the teachers to quickly identify, through the commendation schemes, what a pupil was achieving and what was his/her standing in relation to her/his peers.

Teachers' support of the Scheme resulted in staff agreeing to extend their thinking on the classroom Behaviour Code. A staff team produced a SWIM Code where:

S stood for the standards teachers and pupils were looking for and the expectations which were likely to be fulfilled if the standard was being reached;

W stood for the warning sign which indicated that these standards were not being reached;

I stood for the information base that teachers were using to make their decisions, and

M referred to measures that would be used in order to achieve the standards.

An interesting feature of the SWIM Code was the fact that it offered a simple image of sinking and swimming which everyone could understand. At the time of writing this case study, departments are exploring their use of the SWIM code.

As a marketing feature, the Behaviour Code provided evidence to parents who were considering the school, that the majority of the pupils there were behaving well. The school was able to show that the majority of children were achieving and that there was consistent monitoring through the Award System of the five major ingredients of Classwork, Homework, Attendance, Punctuality and Behaviour. The Cadbury's Award Scheme provided an opportunity for children to be successful across the whole of the ability range. Additionally, the scheme kept parents in contact with their child's progress and attitude to work in school.

Evidence of success

In general:

1 The school's attendance figures improved: over 90 per cent attendance in the Year 10 and 11 cohort and slightly less than 90 per cent attendance throughout the rest of the school. These rates far exceeded previous rates of attendance.

2 HMI noted that 'the school was beginning to change the culture of under-achievement' (*see* also Appendix 4).

3 Recruitment figures went up. Children now travel out of the city to attend Four Dwellings.

4 In relation to parents:
   a) There is a shared language between teacher and parents, i.e. bronze, silver and gold awards are common features of discussions.
   b) At parents' evenings parents ask why their children have only received 19 out of 22 commendations. This has provided the opportunity for a discussion on learning, monitoring pupils' achievements and effort in all the areas of the Award Scheme.
   c) At home the certificates are framed and hung on the wall and if a pupil has received a trophy it is prominently displayed.
   d) Parental attendance at celebratory achievement days has increased. The rewards ceremony attracts on average over 450 people.

5 In relation to staff:
   a) There is evidence of the speedy return of the slips which require colleagues to commend pupils.
   b) There is a general feeling that behaviour has improved within the school and that the SWIM Code is being successful. One department in particular has taken the document, reinterpreted it, providing its own criteria, which is displayed on the walls within its subject area.

6 In relation to pupils :
   a) Pupils have become increasingly engaged in discussion around their achievement.
   b) Staff in their tutor role, allocate a Tuesday evening after school to see children and parents to help pupils with their work.
   c) Catch-up sessions have been initiated where pupils are supported in completing their coursework assignments.
   d) Pupils are better able to succeed and recognise their areas of strength and weakness because of the consistent monitoring within all the areas of the Cadbury Award.

7 To conclude, it is felt that the whole school ethos is now focused on work and achievement. The emphasis on all pupils being commended in some way on the effort they are making in school has motivated and raised levels of pupil commitment to the school. This has had the associated effect of raising pupils' achievements.

Advice to other schools

1 Take small steps to reach long-term aims and goals.
2 Talk to other schools which are succeeding where your school is not.
3 Seek the opinions of pupils to give them a voice. Empower them to take part in the change and improvement process.
4 The same approach is essential with colleagues. It is necessary to hear their opinions through actively seeking them out, checking their desired aims and engaging in continuous monitoring and evaluation.
5 It is important to have colleagues involved who have managerial responsibility to enable the change process to happen.
6 Remember that everything that is put in place will not necessarily be successful.

Reflection and analysis

In analysing this case study some important elements of school improvement are identified which have been highlighted earlier in the book :

1 Pupil involvement

Pupil involvement was important from an early stage. Pupils were engaged in selling their idea to other pupils, staff and the external agent, i.e. Cadbury's. Pupils were committed to the success of the change process, as they saw their ideas put into action. The centrality of their demand was that the award scheme should be 'fair' and that the emphasis should be placed on both achievement and effort related to a pupil's individual potential.

2 Use of external agent

Cadbury's, a large local employer, had provided the scheme with a sense of value and worth. This extended beyond the school into the local community. By funding the awards scheme Cadbury's had given it credibility with both pupils and parents and the wider community.

3 Support and
involvement of
parents

The support of the parents for the project was quite substantial and very public. They attended celebratory evenings and when questioned responded that they felt more involved in 'their school' as a result of the project.

4 Support of
school staff:
development
of collegiality

Within the school commitment from the staff was essential. Initially the main aim had been to win them over to the Cadbury Scheme. It was recognised that the change process could be a slow one and that it could not take place without some level of active participation by the staff. The resulting staff commitment had ensured that the awards and commendations had been given regularly and fairly. Without this immediate support and feedback the project could have failed. As the project gained success, staff supported its extension into further areas of their professional work.

5 Role of the
change agent

The Deputy Head's understanding of the 'process of change' was important to the success of the project. Added to this was his ability as a member of SMT to facilitate change. Furthermore, the enthusiasm and commitment given in his 'leading capacity', coupled with a systematic monitoring of the evidence of success of the scheme, ensured that pupils and staff worked together to support the change process.

APPENDICES TO CASE STUDY B

Appendix 1

The Cadbury Award: How the scheme works

Recognition of achievement

The Cadbury
Award

The Cadbury Awards have been developed to provide encouragement and recognition for effort and achievement. We are grateful for the support and sponsorship given by Cadbury's.

Awards can be achieved for:

1 Attendance
2 Classwork performance
3 Conduct
4 GCSE performance
5 Homework performance
6 Outstanding achievement
7 Outstanding progress
8 Outstanding Tutor Group performance

Attendance Awards are given for the following attendance:

GOLD Award   97%–100%
SILVER Award   94%– 96%
BRONZE Award   90%– 93%

An end-of-year award is given for the standard sustained over two and a half terms from September to the end of May.

Punctuality Awards are given termly for the following level of performance:

GOLD Award   — 0 late arrivals
SILVER Award — 1 late arrival
BRONZE Award — 2 late arrivals

Conduct Awards are given termly and are determined by data collected during the Behaviour Focus Weeks, teacher referrals and tutor comments.

Appendix 1 (contd.)

Classwork and Homework (Years 7 to 9)
Certificates are awarded and parents are informed shortly after.

September–October
November–December
January–April

A total of nine commendations for homework and twelve for classwork can be achieved. When making a recommendation for an award teachers must take into account the effort made relative to ability.

Homework:
GOLD Award   — 9 commendations
SILVER Award   — 8 commendations
BRONZE Award — 7 commendations

Classwork:
GOLD Award   — 12 commendations
SILVER Award   — 11 commendations
BRONZE Award — 10 commendations

The Cadbury Trophy

When a pupil achieves a maximum of 21 commendations he/she is awarded the Cadbury Trophy Level 1 for achievement. (If this award is achieved three times during the school year the pupil keeps the Trophy). The pupil must then aim to achieve the next level of the Cadbury Trophy.

GCSE Coursework Performance (Years 10 and 11)
The allocation of points is related to a seven point scale shown below.

```
1   Is accelerating ahead
2   Is moving up into top gear
3   Is coping with 'the route' in a satisfactory manner
4   Is cruising along, needs to accelerate to arrive on time
5   Has consistently operated in bottom gear
6   Has come to a standstill
7   Is rolling backwards
```

A combination of levels produces a score for the eight subjects studied.

GOLD Award   — 16 points or less
SILVER Award   — 21 points or less
BRONZE Award — 25 points or less

This information is communicated to Parents.

Appendix 1 (contd.)

Outstanding progress and outstanding achievement certificates
These awards are subject-based and are given to pupils who are considered to be making, relative to their ability outstanding progress or achieving a high level. The certificates are issued for the periods:

September–March and April–July

End-of-year awards

The Celebration of Achievement Evening in July is for the presentation of certificates for outstanding performance. To gain these certificates pupils must achieve the following standards.

GOLD Award   — 59/63 commendations
SILVER Award   — 54/58 commendations
BRONZE Award — 51/53 commendations (awarded during Main
                              School Assembly)

In addition other Cadbury Shields are presented to the boys and girls elected as Students of the Year.

'WELL DONE' Voucher
The 'Well Done' Voucher is a means of giving public and instant recognition to achievement. Five vouchers can be exchanged for a certificate which records the achievements written on the vouchers.

All awards should be stored in the pupil's Record of Achievement portfolio after parents have seen them.

These awards are highly valued by pupils, parents, and teachers, and for this reason the Record of Achievement Portfolio should be stored in a very secure place and not left lying around in classrooms.

Appendix 2

Sample of internal awards given which lead to the annual Cadbury Award

Gold	
Silver	
Bronze	

is presented to

_____

of

The Four Dwellings School

for

Homework Performance

September/October 1994

R. Snelldn _____Headteacher

Appendix 2 (contd.) Sample of annual Cadbury Award certificates

THE

Cadbury

AWARD

is presented to

of

The Four Dwellings School

for GCSE Coursework Performance

Signed   *Date*

Cadbury Ltd.

Head Teacher

Appendix 3

Sample of regular letter to pupils and parents

THE FOUR DWELLINGS SCHOOL

DWELLINGS LANE, QUINTON , BIRMINGHAM B32 1RJ

Telephone: 021-422 0131

Fax: 021-423 1352

Headmaster: R. SMOLDON

YEAR 8

May 1994

Dear

It is always a pleasure to congratulate students on their achievements. The boxes with a tick indicate the subjects where the teachers at Four Dwellings are pleased with your homework and classwork performances.

Please remember to talk to your teachers about the boxes where you have not gained a tick. This may indicate a mistake or you may need to find out what you need to do to be commended next time.

Classroom Performance	Subjects	Homework Performance
☐	Art	☐
☐	Drama	
☐	English	☐
☐	French	☐
☐	Geography	☐
☐	History	☐
☐	Mathematics	☐
☐	Music	
☐	Physical Education	
☐	Religious Education	☐
☐	Science	☐
☐	Technology	☐
☐	TOTAL	☐

Yours sincerely

B K SMITH
Head of School

THE Cadbury AWARD

Classroom   Gold/Silver/Bronze

Homework   Gold/Silver/Bronze

Parents/Guardian Signature ....

Date ....

Appendix 4

Extract from OFSTED report: evidence of success

A report from the Office of Her Majesty's Chief Inspector of Schools

**OFFICE FOR STANDARDS
IN EDUCATION**

5. THE QUALITY OF THE SCHOOL AS A COMMUNITY

Behaviour and Discipline

37.   The school is orderly and safe. Most pupils conduct themselves sensibly around the school and in lessons; where they are motivated and engaged in activities, behaviour is good. Relationships between staff and pupils are generally good.

38.   The use of praise and encouragement varies but the careful and systematic monitoring of the school's behaviour code, linked to the commendations and awards scheme which is sponsored by a local industry, has brought improvement in pupils' attitudes. The award system is closely and thoroughly monitored and provides information whereby the school can identify difficulties at an early stage. Pupils whose motivation and attainment give rise to concern may be included in a 'challenge' group which aims to improve relationships and behaviour through a programme of after-school activities and more closely targeted guidance. The award scheme has been in operation for two years and has gained credibility with most pupils and parents. There is now a need to build on this success and to sharpen the criteria for the allocation of rewards, particularly for classwork, homework and conduct, to ensure that commendations are consistently awarded for significant effort and achievement.

41.   The school has begun to develop a regular system of monitoring individual pupils' attendance and punctuality every ten weeks. Commendations are awarded for good attendance and punctuality.

CASE STUDY C

Four Dwellings School

RAISING PUPILS' PERFORMANCE AT GCSE

THE CHALLENGE

The Deputy Head at Four Dwellings had spent considerable time observing teachers in the classroom in both a supportive and a team teaching role. She had developed an awareness that a section of the brightest children were 'under-achieving dramatically' or 'marking time'. Evidence from O level results in 1986, showed that 8 per cent of pupils had received five A to C grades. Despite the 1987 cohort being identified as an abler group than their 1986 counterparts, there had been no improvement from this group in GCSE results. In other words, a talented group had not improved their scores.

Consequently the Deputy asked the question 'What effect was the school having?' From her own experience of the classroom the Deputy felt that:

the work the children were being set wasn't challenging
enough, the pace was slow and when I taught the children
myself, comparing the outputs of those children, to what
they were achieving in other lessons, you knew there was
under-achieving going on.

The new responsibility of being the Curriculum Deputy enabled her to think about a process of positive action to begin to challenge this under-achievement.

Response to the challenge

The Deputy's participation in a Birmingham LEA course entitled 'Quality Development' which involved Higher Education, offered both ideas and approaches. Arguments had to be won with middle managers that under-achievement needed to be recognised. Evidence to show the extent of this under-achievement, which had been gathered in her role as Curriculum Deputy was consequently discussed in a professional and non-threatening collegial context.

With senior management support and acceptance that something needed to be done, the next stage was to identify and explore the issue of under-achievement during a teacher development day. Here staff were involved in identifying pupils in Years 9 and Year 10 who were thought able to achieve D or above in every subject area.

The next stage was to identify a group of 25 pupils in Year 10 who were able to gain 5 Ds and above. There was some flexibility in this choice, however, in that a pupil who might achieve 4 Ds and one E was included in the cohort. It was agreed to hold an off-site conference for the 25 Year-10 pupils who had been identified as the first cohort. Letters to parents which outlined the purpose of this work were the initial stage in the process.

The conference theme titled 'Promoting Achievement, Raising Aspirations' included activities and discussions on themes such as:

1 Five C's opens doors.
2 Reflective analysis of your learning techniques.
3 Reflective analysis of what gets in the way of learning.
4 Strategies for coping with learning and studying.

Discussion with pupils was based on data gathered earlier in the school from logbooks and interviews. Pupils were asked to respond to the question *What do you see getting in the way of your learning?*

Similar on-site conferences were held for all Year 9 and Year 10 pupils. An important feature of all the conferences was that feedback was given to staff, to the whole school through assembly, and was followed up in tutorial time as part of the work on conduct and behaviour. All these activities reinforced a consistent message, which was: *'We can improve'*.

Having selected the cohort, and developed on-site training, the next stage was to provide closer monitoring and targeting of the development of the selected cohort. Both the year tutor and Deputy began a programme with the Year 10 cohort, where they withdrew pupils from lessons for a regular tutorial for ten minutes twice a term. The focus of this discussion was:

a) pupils' work—providing evidence from exercise books and coursework folders
b) pupils' homework—providing evidence from homework logs
c) pupils' attendance records

In these tutorials, pupils discussed serious personal and social difficulties which affected their work or attendance. Others identified practical problems, e.g.:

> I can't do my coursework in this subject because I have
> to go to .... (an external activity), and my mum won't
> let me go out on my own

Another example was:

> I gave in my coursework three months ago and haven't had it back yet.

Other comments involved deadline slippage, which meant three or four pieces of coursework were required at the same time. Surprisingly, in Year 10 many pupils felt that half an hour a night was sufficient for homework. Some pupils admitted that they reguarly did no homework for days on end, and thought this acceptable.

In relation to attendance, pupils were shocked when they were made aware in tutorials that some had lost a total of three weeks out of a school term. Once their attention had been drawn to this pupils responded by reducing their individual absentee levels. The final stage of these tutorials was to direct pupils towards the activities and strategies which were designed to help pupils to improve achievement. The strategies included:

1 Homework guidelines for GCSE, which expected all pupils to allocate two and sometimes three hours a night to homework.
2 An initiative funded by TVEE which enabled the Deputy to invite an outside agency of time management trainers to work with the pupils and help them to produce a personal time manager.
3 Publication of coursework deadlines across departments, which led to a recognition across departments that extending deadlines, whilst it might seem to help pupils, actually caused them greater problems.
4 Coursework catch-up sessions.

When the Year 10 group became Year 11 the tutorials with the year head and Deputy continued and an additional cohort of pupils from Year 10 were targeted in the same way. Within the second year of the initiative further strategies were employed:

- There were voluntary after-school lessons provided by staff.
- The library was re-organised into a resource-based, attractive learning centre.
- Computers were made accessible before, during and after school hours.
- An extra session from an outside agency based on exam techniques, was organised.

Topics covered included:

a) revision techniques
b) study skills
c) how to handle your coursework
d) getting the most out of your teacher.

The study skills focus was then integrated into the whole school tutorial work, thus involving all pupils in Year 10.

However, what was equally important was the continuous reporting back to colleagues, closer monitoring of this particular cohort, and collectors of their own evidence which showed that the initiative was making a difference.

Evidence of success

1 The initiative gained support and was used by teachers working with Year 10 and Year 11 as they began to see increased commitment and achievement by the pupils involved.
2 The Cadbury Award Scheme which used spreadsheets to chart pupils' achievement across five areas (classwork, homework, attendance, punctuality, behaviour) was able to show that the cohort was originally clustered around the bronze commendation and below. In one year, 16 out of 25 pupils had achieved bronze awards and above. This upward shift of the targeted cohort continued to be recorded.
3 Further evidence was gained from the GCSE scores.
   The first cohort 91/92 increased scores from 8 per cent achieving A–C, to 10 per cent achieving A–C.
   The second cohort, 92/93 achieved 13 per cent grades A–C.
   The year 93/94 cohort continued this upward trend with 18 per cent achieving five grades A–C.
   Generally, the percentage of As and Bs also increased. All A–C's moved up at least one grade. The percentage of pupils with GCSE results went up.
4 The partnership between the school and Higher Education manifested itself in a close working relationship between pupils and students studying in HE. For example, pupils undertook a student pursuit during which they participated in the daily life of a university student. During the working day, parents and pupils visited the university together. The collective effect of this liaison was to highlight HE as a realistic and attainable route to a career. For the first time careers destination figures demonstrated an upward trend with pupils actively seeking places in HE.

5 Heads of Department have been made accountable for exam results according to criteria established across the school. Additionally, these are now fed into departmental planning and target setting.

6 Teachers have grown used to providing evidence which they analyse and draw on to inform many aspects of their professional practice. The 'plan, do, review' cycle seems to be firmly in place. The Deputy commented that such procedures *take all the emotional bit out of reporting*. Staff discussions were now based primarily upon objective evidence about pupils, rather than subjective and personal impressions.

7 Departments have started to examine their own classrooms, which has promoted a collegial sharing of policies and teaching strategies. Staff are more willing to try out new ideas and appear to be working more flexibly.

8 An initiative taken by one deputy was reinforced by another deputy through a separate route, i.e. the Cadbury's Scheme, designed to increase, motivate, improve aspirations and meet the challenge to raise GCSE scores.

   For example, both initiatives affected motivation amongst pupils and inspired enthusiasm amongst colleagues. Both deputies shared a commitment that at all stages pupils should be involved, and that any ongoing work must be shared with the whole staff. There was a genuine commitment to developing co-operative collegial ways of working. An important feature of the success of the separate initiatives was the fact that both initiatives supported whole-school improvement.

Advice to other schools

1 One of the most difficult tasks is that of involving parents. Giving parents the option to be involved, is therefore of crucial importance.

2 Schools need to be realistic about the situation they are in. Once schools are realistic about the context in which they find themselves they can then plan how to move forward. As the Deputy Head summarised:

> You have to know your own context really well in a
> very honest way and that sometimes is difficult for
> senior management to do. We need to
> own our situation, warts and all. We need to be prepared
> for bad news . . .

3 It is important to gather and use valid evidence. This was an essential item in taking the argument into departments and to senior manage-

ment. In using this evidence, the Deputy Head established that it was essential they started from a no-blame situation:

> We weren't going to feel guilty or blame anyone. We were going to take an open, honest look at where we were and where we were trying to go forward to from there.

A secure environment in which to handle challenging and sometimes problematic developments is essential if a school is to be honest in appraising its situation.

4   The role of Deputy has to be 'an enabling' role. This may mean that the school's budget needs to be flexibly used to support a push for improvement. Senior management might need to look at certain areas which could provide support for the improvement initiative. These could include resourcing departments, professional development, cover to support a department which is developing new materials or schemes of work. If SMT want the staff to improve they need to support staff in whatever way they can.

5   The process of monitoring pupils is an essential feature of improvement. However, in developing these monitoring procedures it is important that they remain simple.

6   It is essential to involve parents wherever possible, to keep them involved and to widen their understanding of what the school is doing. Providing funds to gather feedback from parents and acting on that feedback is an important means of gaining parental involvement.

Review and analysis section

In analysing this case study there are some important elements of school improvement which have been highlighted earlier in the book:

1 The need to appraise situations honestly prior to change	Any initiative needs to start from a genuine position of honest appraisal of the situation. It should include and hear both pupils' opinions and staff views.
2 Evidence of the need for change	Relevant evaluatory evidence gathered prior to change was an important feature. The sharing of evidence had to occur in a no-blame, secure context.

3 The role of senior management	Initiatives which do not have SMT support or involvement will be less likely to succeed. This is because senior management are channels for communication, have ways of introducing initiatives into all parts of the school, and have direct access to information about learning from the pupils and from the departments and the staff.
4 Monitoring and feedback	The regularity of monitoring and feedback, the focus on praising pupils' achievements according to their merit maintained pupil motivation. The issue itself of raising standards was essentially an uncontroversial issue amongst the staff. This project showed that where established routines for monitoring pupil progress existed, pupil achievements were enhanced.
5 Role of external agents	The role played by HE as an external agent in the process of change was important because it positively affected pupils' perceptions of their own capabilities and expectations.
6 Learning how to learn	The Conference entitled 'Promoting Achievement: Raising Aspirations' focused on the language and process of learning. Its content was based upon the pupils' own experiences of learning effectively at school and the process explored and shared that understanding. The conference generated a language about effective learning and confidence about learning which pupils could more readily articulate.They learned to understand their own learning processes and were more able to devise strategies to assist them in their future study.
7 Learning styles	The conferences and tutorials had the combined effect of making implicit learning explicit, by engaging learners in different modes of learning.
8 Active learning time	In an attempt to maximise the time pupils spent engaged in learning, additional sessions were provided for pupils at lunchtime and after school. A homework room was provided, computer access was extended and the library became an attractive resource for after-school learning.

APPENDIX TO CASE STUDY C

Appendix 1

Extract from OFSTED report: evidence of success

A report from the Office of Her Majesty's Chief Inspector of Schools

**OFFICE FOR STANDARDS
IN EDUCATION**

3.   STANDARDS AND QUALITY ACHIEVED

Standards of Achievement

25.   The school has taken some positive steps to tackle underachievement in GCSE examinations through a quality development initiative. Individual pupils who show the ability to achieve higher standards at GCSE are offered an appropriate supportive programme to raise expectations. This aims to broaden the horizons of post-sixteen opportunities, to improve study skills and provide guidance to parents and pupils about ways in which further progress can be made. This initiative also provides some additional classes for pupils prior to examinations in Y11. The programme has helped to raise expectations and awareness of the importance of achievement throughout the school. Initial evaluation shows some improvements in attendance and the standard of these pupils' achievement has at least, been maintained. In the longer-term, success will depend on embedding the more succesful features of the work into the delivery of the curriculum for all pupils.

REFERENCES AND FURTHER READING

Adey, P. and Shayer, M. (1990) 'Accelerating the development of formal thinking in middle and high school students', *Journal of Research in Science Teaching*, **27**, pp 267–85.

Anderson, L.W. (ed) (1984) *Time and School Learning*, London, Croom Helm.

Ausubel, D.P. (1968) *Educational Psychology: A Cognitive View*, New York, Holt, Rinehart and Winston.

Beare, H., Caldwell, J. and Millikan, R. (1989) *Creating an Excellent School*, London, Routledge.

Beare, H., Caldwell, B. and Millikan, R. (1993) 'Leadership', in Preedy, M. (ed) (1993) *Managing the Effective School*, London, Paul Chapman in conjunction with the Open University.

Belbin, R.M. (1981) *Management Teams: Why They Succeed and Fail*, Oxford, Heinemann.

Bennett, N. (1976) *Teaching Styles and Pupil Progress*, London, Open Books.

Bennett, N. (1991) 'The quality of classroom learning experiences for children with special educational needs' in Ainscow, M. (ed), *Effective Schools for All*, London, Heinemann.

Bickel, E. and Bickel, D.D. (1986) 'Effective schools, classrooms and instruction: implications for special education', *Exceptional Children*, **52** (6), pp 489–500.

Brandes, D. and Ginnis, P. (1986) *A Guide to Student-Centred Learning*, Oxford, Basil Blackwell.

Bransford, J.D., Stein, B.S., Arbitman-Smith, R. and Vye, N.J. (1985) 'Three approaches to improving thinking and learning', in Segal, J.W., Chipman, S.F. and Glaser, R. (eds), *Thinking and Learning Skills: Relating Instruction to Basic Research*, Vol 1, Hillsdale, NJ, Erlbaum.

Brophy, J.E. (1983) 'Classroom organisation and management', *The Elementary School Journal*, **82**, pp 266–85.

Brown, S., Ridell, S. and Duffield, J. (1995) 'Possibilities and problems of small-scale studies to unpack the findings of large-scale school effectiveness' in Gray, J., Reynolds, D., Fitz-Gibbon, C. and Jesson, D. (eds) *Merging Traditions: The Future of Research on School Effectiveness and School Improvement*, London, Cassell.

Bruner, J.S. (1960) *The Process of Education*, Cambridge, Mass., Harvard University Press.

Calderhead, J. (ed) (1988) *Teachers' Professional Learning*, London, Falmer Press.

Caldwell, B. and Spinks, J. (1992) *Leading the Self Managing School*, London, Lawrence Erlbaum Associates.

Carraher, T.N., Carraher, D.W. and Schliemann, A.D. (1985) 'Mathematics in the streets and in schools', *British Journal of Developmental Psychology*, **3**, pp 21–9.

Carroll, J.B. (1989) 'The Carroll Model: a 25 year retrospective and prospective view', *Educational Researcher*, **18**, pp 26–31.

Claxton, G. (1984) *Live and Learn: An Introduction to the Psychology of Growth and Change in Everyday Life*, London, Open Univesity Press.

Claxton, G. (1990) *Teaching to Learn; a Direction for Education*, London, Cassell.

Coker, H., Medley, D., Soar, R. and Stoney, S. M. (1988) *Perspectives on TVEI. A set of papers exploring management themes within TVEI*, Slough, NFER.

Coleman, J.S., Campbell, E., Hobson, C., McPartland, J., Mood, A., Weinfeld, F. and York, R. (1966) *Equality of Educational Opportunity*, Washington, Natural Centre for Educational Statistics.

Corno, L. (1979) 'Classroom instruction and the matter of time' in Duke, D. L. (ed), *Classroom Management* (78th yearbook of the National Society for the Study of Education), Chicago, NSSE.

Creemers, B.P.M. (1994) *The Effective Classroom*, London, Cassell.

Crosby, P.B. (1986) *Quality without Tears: The Art of Hassle Free Management*, New York, McGraw-Hill.

Cullingford, C. (ed) (1985) *Parents, Teachers and Schools*, London, Robert Royce.

Dale, R. (1990) *The TVEI Story*, Buckingham, Open University Press.

Deming, W.E. (1986) *Out of the Crisis*, Cambridge, Mass., MIT, Centre for Advanced Engineering Study.

Department for Education (1993) *Effective Management in Schools*, London, HMSO.

Devine, M., Mingard, S., Black, H. and Fenwick, S. (1994) 'School for Skills. A national survey of the development through TVEI of personal and transferable skills', Edinbugh, SCRE.

Doyle, W. (1987) 'Research on teaching effects as a resource for improving instruction', in Wideen, M. and Andrews, I. (eds), *Staff Development for School Improvement*, Lewes, Falmer Press.

Driver, R. (1983) *The Pupil as Scientist*, Milton Keynes, Open University Press.

Dweck, C. and Repucci, N. (1973) 'Learned helplessness and reinforcement responsibility in children', *Journal of Personality and Social Psychology*, **25**, pp 109–16.

Eggleston, J.F., Galton, M.J. and Jones, M.E. (1976) *Processes and Products of Science Teaching*, London, Macmillian.

English, T. and Harris, A. (1992) *An Evaluation Toolbox For Schools*, London, Longman.

Entwistle, N. (1987) *Understanding Classroom Learning*, London, Hodder and Stoughton.

Entwistle, N. (1988) *Styles of Learning and Teaching*, London, David Fulton Publishers.

Everard, B. and Morris, G. (1990) *Effective School Management*, London, Paul Chapman.

Fitz-Gibbon, C.T. (1991) 'Multilevel modelling in an indicator system', in Raudenbush, S. and Willms, J.D. (eds), *Schools, Classrooms and Pupils*, San Diego, Academic Press.

Fitz-Gibbon, C.T. (1992) 'School effects at A level—genesis of an information system', in Reynolds, D. and Cuttance, P. (eds), *School Effectiveness: Research Policy and Practice*, London, Cassell.

Fitz-Gibbon, C.T., Tymms, P.B. and Hazelwood, R.D. (1990) 'Performance indicators and information systems', in Reynolds, D., Creemers, B.P.M. and Peters, T. (eds), *School Effectiveness and School Improvement*, Groningen, RION.

Fullan, M.G. (1988) *What's Worth Fighting For in the Principalship: Strategies for Taking Charge in the Elementary School Principalship*, Toronto, Ontario Public School Teachers' Federation.

Fullan, M.G. (1991) *The New Meaning of Educational Change*, London, Cassell.

Fullan, M.G. (1992) *Successful School Improvement*, Buckingham, Open University Press.

Fullan, M.G. and Hargreaves, A. (1991) *What's Worth Fighting For: Working Together for Your School*, Toronto, Ontario Public School Teachers' Federation.

Gagne, R. M. (1985) *The Conditions of Learning and Theory of Instruction*, New York, Holt, Rinehart and Winston.

Gleeson, D. (ed) (1987) *TVEI and Secondary Education: a Critical Appraisal*, Milton Keynes, Open University Press.

Gray, J. (1993) 'The Quality of Schooling: Frameworks for Judgement', in Preedy, M. (ed) op. cit.

Greenfield, T. B. (1986) 'Leaders and Schools: Wilfulness and non-natural order in organisations', in Sergiovanni, T.J. and Corbally, J.E. (eds), *Leadership and Organisational Culture: New Perspectives on*

Administrative Theory and Practice, Chicago, University of Chicago Press.

Haertel, G.D. Walberg, H.J. and Weinstein, T. (1983) 'Psychological models of educational performance: A theoretical synthesis of constructs', *Review of Educational Research*, **53**, pp 75–91.

Hargreaves, A. and Fullan, M.G. (1992) *Understanding Teacher Development*, New York, Cassell.

Harris, A. and Russ, J. (1994a) *Pathways to School Improvement*, Moorfoot, TEED, Dept of Employment.

Harris, A. and Russ, J. (1994b) *The Learning School: A Pathway to Real School Improvement*, paper presented at annual BEMAS conference, Manchester.

Harris, A., Jamieson, I.M. and Russ, J. (1995) 'A study of effective departments in secondary schools', *School Organisation*, **15**, 3.

Heene, J. and Schulsmans, K. [1988] 'Teacher's effectiveness: the "grey-box", in McAlpine, A., Brow, S. and Kentley, E. (eds), *New Challenges for Teachers and Teacher Education*, Amsterdam, Swets and Zeitlinger.

Hilgard, E.R. (1963) 'A perspective on the relationships of learning theory and education practice', *Theories of Learning and Instruction*, Chicago, National Society for the Study of Education, 63rd Yearbook.

HMI, (1977) *Ten Good Schools*, London, HMSO.

Holly, P. and Southworth, G. (1989) *The Developing School*, London, Falmer Press.

Holt, J. (1984) *How Children Fail*, Harmondsworth, Penguin.

Hopkins, D. (1986) 'The Change Process and Leadership in Schools', *School Organisation*, **6**, 1, pp 26–34.

Jencks, C.S., Smith, M., Ackland, H., Bane, M.J., Cohen, D., Gintis, H., Heyns, B. and Micholson, S. (1972) *Inequality: A Re-assessment of the Effect of Family and Schooling in America*, New York, Holt, Rinehart and Winston.

Jenkins, H.O. (1991) *Getting it Right: a Handbook for Successful School Leadership*, Oxford, Blackwell.

Jesson, D., Gray, J. and Tranmer, M. (1992) 'GCSE Performance in Nottinghamshire 1991: Pupil and School Factors', Nottinghamshire LEA (mimeo).

Joyce, B. and Showers, B. (1991) *Information-Processing: Models of Teaching*, Aptos, CA, Booksend Laboratories.

Juran, J. (1979) *Quality Control Handbook*, 3rd edition, New York, McGraw-Hill.

Kounin, J.S. (1970) *Discipline and Group Management in Classrooms*, New York, Holt, Rinehart and Winston.

Kyriacou, C. (1986) *Effective Teaching in Schools*, Oxford, Basil Blackwell.

Levine, D. and Lezotte, C. (1990) 'Unusually Effective schools: A Review and Analysis of Research and Practice', *International Journal of Educational Research*, **13**, 7, pp 815–25.

Lieberman, A. (1986) 'Collaborative Research: Working with not working on', *Educational Leadership*, **37**, 5, pp 379–86.

Little, J.W. (1990) 'The persistence of privacy: autonomy and initiative in teachers' professional relations', *Teachers College Record*, **9**, 4, pp 509–36.

Louis, K.S. and Miles, M. (1990) *Improving the Urban High School*, New York, Teachers College Press.

Macbeth, J. (1993) 'Parent–teacher partnership: a minimum programme and a signed understanding', in Preedy, M. (ed), op. cit.

Marton, F. (1975) 'How students learn', in Entwistle, N.J. and Hounsell, D. (eds) *How Students Learn*, Lancaster, University of Lancaster.

Marton, F., Hounsell, D. and Entwistle, N. (eds) (1984) *The Experience of Learning*, Edinburgh, Scottish Academic Press.

Marton, F. and Saljo, R. (1976) 'On qualitative differences in learning', *British Journal of Educational Psychology*, **46**, 2, pp 4–11.

McPherson, A. (1992) *Measuring Added Value in Schools: NCE Briefing No 1*, London, National Commission on Education.

Maslow, A.H. (1968) 'Some educational implications of the humanistic psychologies', *Harvard Educational Review*, **38**, pp 685–96.

Miles, M. (1986) 'Research Findings on the Stages of School Improvement', New York, Centre for Policy Research (mimeo).

Mills, A.R. and Murgatroyd, S. (1991) *Organisational Rules: A Framework for Understanding Organisational Action*, Milton Keynes, Open University Press.

Mortimore, P. (1995) 'School Effectiveness and the Management of Effective Learning and Teaching', *School Effectiveness and School Improvement*, **4**, 4, pp 290–310.

Mortimore, P. and MacBeath, J. (1994) 'Quest for the secrets of success', *Times Educational Supplement*, No 4056, March 25, p 14.

Mortimore, P., Sammons, P., Stoll, L., Lewis, D. and Ecob, R. (1988) *School Matters: The Junior Years*, Somerset, Open Books.

Murgatroyd, S. (1992) School Effectiveness and School Structuring: a comparative analysis of two lines of school improvement. Paper presented at the International Congress for School Effectiveness and School Improvements, Victoria, British Columbia, Canada.

Murgatroyd, S. and Morgan, C. (1993) *Total Quality Management and the School*, Milton Keynes, Open University Press.

National Commission on Education (1995) *Success Against the Odds: Effective Schools in Disadvantaged Areas*, London, Routledge.

Nias, J., Southworth, G. and Campbell, P. (1992) *Whole School Curriculum Development in Primary Schools*, London, Falmer Press.

OFSTED (1993) *Access and Achievement in Urban Education*, London, HMSO.

OFSTED (1992a, 1994a) (revised) *Framework for the Inspection of Schools*, London, HMSO.

OFSTED, (1992b, 1994b) (revised), *Handbook for the Inspection of Schools*, London, HMSO.

Otts, J.S. (1989) *The Organisational Culture Perspective*, Pacific Gore, CA, Brook Cole.

Pea, R.D. (1989) *Socialising the Knowledge Transfer Problem*, Report No 1RL89–0009 Palo Alto, CA, Institute for Research on Learning.

Peters, T.J. and Waterman, R.H. (1982) *In Search of Excellence: Lessons from America's best Run Companies*, New York, Harper and Row.

Piaget, J. (1972) *Psychology and Epistemology*, Harmondsworth, Penguin.

Porter, A.C. and Brophy, J.E. (1988) *The Social World of the Primary School*, London, Cassell.

Preedy, M. (1993) (ed) *Managing the Effective School*, Paul Chapman Publishing in association with Open University Press, London.

Purkey, S.C. and Smith, M.S. (1985) 'School Reform: the district policy implications of the effective schools literature', *The Elementary School Journal*, **85**, 6, pp 45–56.

Reynolds, D. (1985) *Studying School Effectiveness*, Basingstoke, Falmer Press.

Reynolds, D. and Cuttance, P. (1992) *Schools Effectiveness Research: Policy and Practice*, London, Cassell.

Rosenholtz, S.J. (1989) *Teacher's Workplace: The Social Organisation of Schools*, New York, Longman.

Rosenshine, B. (1983) 'Teaching functions in instructional programs', *The Elementary School Journal* **83**, 4, pp 335–51.

Rutter, M., Maughan, B., Mortimore, P. and Ouston, J. (1979) *Fifteen Thousand Hours*, London, Open Books.

Sammons, P., Thomas, S. and Mortimore, P. (1995) 'Accounting for variations in academic effectiveness between schools and departments,' Paper presented at ECER Conference, Bath.

Saunders, L. and Schargen, I. (1995) *QUASE: A Value Added Measure*, Slough, NFER.

Scheerens, J. (1992) *School Effectiveness*, London, Casssell.

Schein, E.H. (1985) *Organisational Culture and Leadership*, Jossey-Bass, San Francisco.

Schon, D. (1971) *Beyond the Stable State*, London, Temple Smith.

Schon, D.A. (1983) *The Reflective Practitioner*, London, Temple Smith.

Shanker, A. (1990) 'Here we stand', *The New York Times*, July 8th, p E7.

Skinner, B.F. (1954) 'The science of learning and the art of teaching', *Harvard Educational Review,* **24**, pp 88–97.

Smith, D. and Tomlinson, S. (1989) *The School Effect: A study of Multi-Racial Comprehensives*, London, Policy Studies Institute.

Southworth, G. (1990) 'Leadership and effective primary schools', *School Organisation*, **10**, 1, pp 3–16.

Southworth, G. (1994) 'The Learning School,' in Ribbins, P. and Burridge, E. (eds) *Improving Education Promoting Quality in Schools*, London, Cassell.

Steedman, J. (1980) *Progress in Secondary Schools*, London, National Children's Bureau.

Stenhouse, L. (1975) *An Introduction to Curriculum Research and Development*, London, Heinemann.

Stogdill, R.M. (1974) *Handbook of Leadership*, New York, The Free Press.

Stoll, L. and Fink, D. (1992) 'Effecting School Change: The Halton Approach', *School Effectiveness and School Improvement*, **3**, 1, pp 19–41.

Stricht, T. (1989) 'Adult literacy Education' in Rothkopf, E.Z. (ed), *Review of Research in Education 1988–89*, **15**, Washington, DC, American Educational Research Association.

Van Velzen, W. *et al* (1985) *Making School Improvement Work*, Leuven, ACCO.

Walberg, H. (1990) 'Productive teaching and instruction: assessing the knowledge base', *Phi Delta Kappan*, **71**, 6, pp 470–8.

Wang, M. C. (1991) 'Adaptive instruction: an alternative approach to providing for pupil diversity', in Ainscow, M. (ed), *Effective Schools for All*, London, Fulton.

Waterhouse, P. (1990) *Classroom Management*, Stafford, Network Educational Press.

White, R. (1959) 'Motivation reconsidered: the concept of competence', *Psychological Review,* **66**, pp 297–333.

Wood, R. and Bandura, A. (1989) 'Impact of conceptions of ability on self-regulating mechanisms and complex decision-making', *Journal of Personality and Social Psychology*, **56**, pp 407–15.

Woods, P. (1990) *Teacher Skills and Strategies*, Philadelphia, Falmer Press.

INDEX